# THE NAMED AND THE NAMELESS

PEN AMERICA

2018 PRISON WRITING AWARDS ANTHOLOGY

THE NAMED AND THE NAMELESS

2018 Prison Writing Awards Anthology

First edition

For additional questions regarding reproduction, quotation, or to request a pdf for review contact prisonwriting@pen.org

**Published by:** PEN America

**Book Design by:** Caits Meissner and Robert Pollock

**Cover Image by:** Molly Crabapple

**Cover Design by:** Caits Meissner, Robert Pollock, and Nadxieli Nieto

**Typefaces:** Bell MT, Neutraface Text, Have Heart Two, Courier Prime, and Source Sans Pro

**ISBN-10:** 1725981157

**ISBN-13:** 978-1725981157

# Notes

The Honorable Mention prose and drama pieces appear in these pages as excerpts. All the work featured in this anthology, along with the author biographies, can be read in full on PEN America's website by visiting the Prison Writing Contest archive at pen.org/prison-writing.

Founded in 1971, the PEN Prison Writing Program believes in the restorative, rehabilitative and transformative possibilities of writing. We provide hundreds of imprisoned writers across the country with free writing resources, skilled mentors, and audiences for their work. Our program supports free expression, and encourages the use of the written word as a legitimate form of power. We strive towards an increasingly integrative approach, aiming to amplify the voices and writing of imprisoned people to expand beyond the silo of prison, and identity of prisoner.

*The Prison Writing Contest Prizes are sponsored by the generous support of the Greenburger Center for Social & Criminal Justice.*

*Programming for PEN America's Prison Writing Program is made possible in part by generous funding from the Stavros Niarchos Foundation.*

# Contents

**ILLUSTRATIONS**

Prison is honest. I can say anything here,
as long as I'm willing to get punched in the face.

**—Edward Ji**

# Introduction
## CAITS MEISSNER AND ROBERT POLLOCK

As a new team, we came into PEN America's Prison Writing Program just as the winners of our annual Prison Writing Contest had been decided, and it was our honor and pleasure to package, sign and send the congratulatory letters. With predictable frequency, many of the letters we send come back to us emblazoned with the yellow sticker of return-to-sender. Usually mail is returned due to one of many prison correspondence issues. With the hundreds of letters and submissions we receive monthly, we are used to inventing creative ways of handling boomerang mail. This time, the label read deceased. Michael Lambrix, our third place winner in the nonfiction essay category, was executed on death row in the time between submitting his manuscript and winning the prize.

This sobering moment opened up a series of questions that guide our daily work: How do we respect the gravity of the stories we receive? How do we support the voices of those vanished from our society through incarceration? In what ways do the contributions of marginalized writers enrich, challenge, and improve our understanding of the world? Written from the last cell before death, Lambrix's story exposes the possibility for empathy and compassion to be uncovered within an unimaginable moment of mortal terror. As we are continually faced with the intensity of an unrelentingly punitive and draconian prison system, as well as the complexity and confronting nature of crime itself, Lambrix's story reminds us of the urgency to bear witness to the overwhelming spectrum of the human experience, even—perhaps especially—the most difficult parts.

After over 30 years of incarceration, Alejo Da'wud Rodriguez, a four-time winner of our contest, opened our Break Out: Voices From Inside event at the 2018 World Voices Festival, where we showcased the work from the Prison Writing Contest archives. He spoke powerfully about the strange relief he felt on his first night in prison, reaching out to touch the four walls boxing him in. For the first time in his life, he was able to see and feel the walls that had been erected metaphorically, long before his arrest. Angel Ayala, a member of our mentor program, allowed us to share a letter where he described the process of self-reflection within those walls:

> You know how in our brains we have these "mirror cells," which make us smile when others smile, or subconsciously mirror the face and emotions we see? I think that for people in captivity, who are deprived of normal interactions and have very limited human contact, they begin to mirror the metal and cement, its grayness, coldness, its blank lifelessness—and we mirror the cell, we become cells, which are hollow and gray and designed to destroy humanity.

Though prison, and the people it houses, are removed from public view, prisons—spiritually, metaphorically—are also everywhere. And though the experience of incarceration is a distinct one, the emotions expressed are universal, though often rendered in high definition hyper-reality. Our contest-winning works range from harrowing to gut-bustingly funny. We read horror stories that move us to our core about institutionalized violence, brutal conditions, and the systemic issues that shamefully position America as the world's leading incarcerator. But what buoys these writings are the threads of connection interwoven in the text: unlikely friendships, the birds outside the window, family returning, redemption, self-reflection, tremendous transformation. How do we also uplift the joy and beauty expressed in the writing we receive? Though all of these writers are writing from prison, they are, of course, unique, complex individuals with dynamic and vibrant identities and expression. This is why we view our work as a connective experience, rather than a charitable one, where reciprocal learning, sharing, and growth occur. As our mirror cells indicate, it is imperative that we stay engaged with each other's humanity for the health of our emotional lives and the health of our greater society.

Our contest is deliberated over by the Prison Writing Committee, who have judged thousands of manuscripts over the years, some members for over two decades. The Committee readers offer tremendous time, care, and energy to not only identify the winners, but to write personal messages of encouragement and comments to non-winners. Among the non-winners, the Committee looks for earnest and ambitious new writers who can be directed to the mentorship program. The dedication and commitment of the Prison Writing Committee is the engine of this entire operation.

It is the first year we are presenting these winners without the longtime guidance of Jackson Taylor and Tim Small, who worked with unwavering commitment to support and amplify the voices of incarcerated writers through the PEN Prison Writing Program. The program's reputation within the prison arts movement is unparalleled as an early innovator, and it is a deeply meaningful experience for many writers behind the walls. It is no small task to create a system of engagement in a landscape nearly completely devoid of technology. Operating through mailed letters, Jackson and Tim orchestrated this program into what we see today. In a transition meeting, Jackson shared his guiding question: What is best for the men and women we work with? It is this care and intention that allowed the beloved and transformative program to touch so many lives. We are grateful to Jackson and Tim for creating this powerful legacy, and we're proud to carry their work forward.

For the first time in the contest's history, we are excited that in your hands is a full print anthology of our winning work, and we hope you will bring your full humanity to the reading. We invite you to share responses to the work with us to, in turn, share with the writers in prison by emailing it to prisonwriting@pen.org. It cannot be underestimated how meaningful it is to receive feedback, especially behind the walls.

Read on!

Caits Meissner, Prison and Justice Writing Program Manager
Robert Pollock, Prison Writing Program Coordinator

# FICTION

*First Place*

# Richard
## WILLIAM MYRL SMITHERMAN

The shadow man first came to Richard on the day that he was raped. In memory, the two events conflate. So it is not that the shadows flowed out of the cracks in his spirit, like ants flowing out of a crack in the kitchen floor, or that what was done to him was done because he was already somehow ruined inside and therefore guilty. It was both.

It was Richard's job to gather eggs in the morning. He wasn't big enough to bring water in from the pump or do much else besides tangle in his mother's night dress as she busied herself with breakfast. The coop was dark like the caves higher in the mountain where he wasn't meant to be playing, dark like the secret places in himself and the echoing unknowns of behind-door adult choices. The coop was the mouth of a monster, stinking with a different stink in the dry and in the wet, clean with the filth of feathers and excess rubbish from the gentle raptors that resided there. He crouched to enter, though he was small enough to stand erect beneath the little door. He would try and surprise the birds, but he couldn't. They clucked and bawked at him like they had seen it before and he was no one anyhow so why bother.

Acrid and acid with the straw in need of changing and the closed close air of the monster's throat, warm despite the chill of night. It assailed him with all that was familiar and certain and safe. This was a thing both necessary and enjoyed, a prelude to the flaking half-baked biscuits with a drizzle of fresh honey. The birds looked to him and he to them as a sign that the day was soon arriving.

In the predawn unlight, he navigated by touch as rough wood gave way to yielding pulsing layers and admonitory clucks before his hand closed around the firm ovoid and grey black prizes. The sun had yet to pierce the slats of the coop and transform them into brown or speckled shells. He piled them in a basket. The birds knew him, and he had named them all—Fatbutt and No Bones and Charlie—and they responded to his coos and calls as he made his round in the warm throat of the beast.

Out of the darkness he came, bearing treasures into the kitchen where the slate wreath of dawn had just begun to penetrate. Daddy was asleep and would remain so until midday, and Uncle Fred, who couldn't find a home of his own or a family to keep there, had gone out the night before and not returned. It was a perfect morning, and Richard washed his hands and face without complaining that one or the other would have been sufficient. Daddy had fashioned a chair so Richard could sit high at the table like the adults did. He had made the table as well and the cabinets and sundry other artifacts unbeautiful but clean and robust because he was a maker of things and not an artist, and there was a timeless difference between the two. Daddy was a carpenter, but today was Saturday and there would be no going into town.

How it was that birds took in feed and produced food was as miraculous and commonplace as the way seeds grew into saplings, into tender creaking giants into splintery play castles, into mulch, and seeds, and soil. These were facts of the world not to be questioned, as fundamental as mother cooking breakfast or daddy sleeping in or why he had to ride into town to go to school while the other children seemed to live there.

The eggs were fried beside the biscuits, an enormous plate wider than his outstretched hands. He ate it because he was a hero and would need his strength one day if he was going to be a man alone living in the mountain with the bears. When he was finished he helped his mother with the clearing. She ate standing by the stove because a mother's schedule did not permit for chairs. He swept out from under her feet so he could sweep the porch as he did every morning as the sun warmed the gravid swollen earth, and he watched for black snakes. The dark beneath the house had given birth once before at his urging to a line of shimmering shade that vanished in the grass and made him gape with wonder.

The car, without its dusty roar, was silent in the open shed beside the house, beside the tools and rusted cans with their jags of wounding teeth. Richard used the broom to check beneath the car for snakes, stymied again for the dark was greedy and unwilling to create. Chores finished, the morning was still fresh and he knew the mountain would be coming slow alive.

He went ranging in the woods beyond his house, the gentle rise of moss-ribboned soil and stones exposed like bones of ancient and forgotten things. The trees were vast and immemorial ponderers of skyline that welcomed him with grazing leaves and the scents of rich decay. He crawled among the roots, a vole searching for a meal, a serpent birthing out of shadow, hungry as the nothing it was made within. In the forest, as in darkness, there were always some things darting in the corners of his eyes: animal, or man, or angels people prayed to. Birds unlike his cluckers raced riffing peals of song among the elder boughs. He has tried to catch them many times, no different than to try to catch their voices in his hands. Still he climbs, willful and uncaring of the danger, without courage but with glowing ignorance of evil and of wrong. His hands cling to rough bark and shaking limb, tug at shaking limb to draw him up as high as nests and dreams. He is not a fox or serpent simple in its hungers; he is a man who longs for ownership with all its viscous, vicious consequences. Steady till the branch below him cracks and he must shimmy backward out of reach of those most potent promises. He knows the eggs up high will one day hatch to singing wonders, while the ones he catches in his basket give life to his breakfast alone. He has planted them before in holes that the mysterious powers of dark and soil would raise a sapling from the egg. They never do.

Somehow the soil knows the nature of what is hid within so that it makes seeds into trees and eggs into birds but not all eggs. The soil watches him like the birds do. It knows him like they do. The trees are friendly even when they scratch his hands, and they love him and he them because they are his friends and they would tell him if there was something wrong. The shadows flitting in the corners of his eyes want to tell him something different. He doesn't listen to them. The smell of good decay is not so different from the smell of bad, and sometimes poison germs inside of sweet raw eggs make him sick, so he doesn't eat them raw no more except when he is hungry.

He has lived this way forever, and it will never change.

A fox was in the woods today, or he thought he saw a fox. He had to climb to see it clearly, and it flees when he comes near. The shadow underneath it flies farther than a hair in the wind, and it looks back at him as if to ask why he doesn't follow so he does.

The fox is sure and quick, and him, with the handicap of human hands and feet, stumbling over rocks and tearing through unhappy brambles. The fox and the boy have not met, but they are not afraid to meet because the cracks in the clay of their spirits that make strangers horrible have yet to harden into permanence.

The fox escapes when the forest breaks, vanishing into grass. It has led him to a place he knows he should not be. There is a massive stump in the clearing, with a lid fashioned by his father's hand, serviceable, durable, without flourish. There is water in the stump that makes his daddy and his uncle Fred sick, though they drink it anyway. His uncle is lying on the ground beside the stump, and he looks dead like an egg from the cluckers.

Richard goes to him.

Uncle Fred doesn't move when Richard comes near, so he looks inside the stump. The lid isn't all the way shut, and he can smell the poison of decay and sharp cool liquid that he knows he should not touch.

"Wanna try it?" His uncle is still on the ground with his eyes open and glassy and his mouth moves like a corpse's mouth releasing gas. "Nobody here but us."

Richard didn't say anything, didn't leave either, and that was choice enough. Fred dipped a wooden mug into the still and brought clear liquid out of the darkness. He pressed it against Richard's mouth and grabbed his shoulder so he couldn't twist away. The liquid was cool, and it burned his throat so bad he coughed and spilled it.

"Look what you did," Uncle Fred said. "You're a damn mess." He made Richard drink it until he started to cry and his head was hot with fuzz and bees.

"This isn't what you wanted?" Uncle Fred smelled like the bad sort of decay. "Why'd you come out here then?"

He drew Richard to him into the enveloping pungency of drink and stale sweat. Richard was afraid to move. His Uncle seemed to sleep again, with his arm around him as immovable as the earth beneath reminding him that he was a child who was powerless when adults chose to make him so. Then a hand was on his leg, and the hot breath on the back of his head was telling him to lie still.

Once, Richard had touched the stove while it was hot from cooking and burned his fingers so they swelled and filled with liquid clear as that in the still. So it was true that the darkness inside of him was the same as the darkness of the stump in the woods, because they made the same things. He remembered that flame, how bright it had felt like a flash of light that filled his whole body with the spark to run and how he had cried because he was little then and it was alright for little ones to cry. Touching fire may have been his first memory; and it was converging with the present instance, which was a future memory, like a scar in the wet lightning of his skull.

His pants were down. The fire filled him and tore him, and he could not pull his hand away this time. When it was finished, Uncle Fred said he was doing it to punish Richard for being willful and drinking from the still when he knew he wasn't meant to, and he wasn't to tell his mom or dad because if dad found out he would have to punish Richard just like Fred had done and mom would tell dad he knew because she always told if he pushed her or hit her she would tell him anything he wanted. But he could tell them, Uncle Fred would, so they understand he had already been punished enough and didn't need no more. Wait a while and come on home and everything would work out fine.

His uncle left him beside the still, laying in the grass on his side with his pants crumpled around his feet, and he continued to lay there waiting for the burning to stop but it was worse than the time he had touched the stove because it didn't stop and he couldn't even see that part of himself to know if it was blistering because it was supposed to be dark there.

One of his shadows was standing at the edge of the clearing plain as if it were a man. Why he could see it now and not before when it had always been on the edge of his eyes was a question in want of an answer. But when he looked away and back it remained, and he knew it would follow him home.

Richard was sick beside the still. Then he felt himself, and there was blood. So he rinsed in a rill that ran above the house where he had caught a minnow once by letting it swim into his hands. The day was changing, and its strength was like the strength of adults in that there was nothing you could do about it and you had to make adjustments. This was still his mountain, and his life was in the earth. He thought about burying himself somehow so that he would be like the eggs that he had buried, dead and sick inside with no roots growing because the soil knew what was good and meant to grow, like seeds, which he wasn't.

It was afternoon when he made his way back down to the house. The trees would not speak to him. His father said nothing, but cuffed him hard so that he stumbled. His mother looked at him and shook her head and told him to get washed up and go to bed without his supper. Minutes later, or maybe longer, he was laying on his side again with a rag for the bleeding. He didn't want to make a mess of his bedding and be in more trouble. The darkness welled around him with a heavy mass of bitter shadows, comforting and comfortless. They had seen it and they had not saved him because he deserved it. Because he was guilty, they could show him what they truly were—the shades of his own sin, the missed prayers and stolen eggs buried in the ground, the curses he'd repeated, and the thoughts he wasn't meant to have—and they told him it wasn't over. Because he had been punished meant he would be punished again. He had not changed, he would not grow, he was the thing that died when it was born and hid beneath the shadows of the porch and vanished in the grass.

*Second Place*

# An Ungodly Godlike Man

## PETER M. DUNNE

*Slay the master.*

You will never be the master if you never kill your idols. *Never.* You will always remain a slave. That's what I was told as a child, and that's what I live by. It's a universal truth. A piece of code embedded in the soul at birth. Hold up—let me stop: I don't believe in silly things like the soul. I don't *believe*, period. To believe is to lie. Not just to others, but to yourself. And that's just stupid, isn't it? It's the equivalent of me calling myself 'God's gift to Atheism.' I'm not an atheist; I believe in myself. I know this sounds strange after what I just said, but it's true.

Okay, I'm lying.

See?

See how that works?

Like a pearl accreting around dirt, we've built ourselves around these lies. Lies which soil the psyche, tarnish the world behind our eyes. My eyes tell the truth. If you could look inside my head, however, you'd sour like bad milk; but, then again, sour milk *is* one of the main ingredients in yogurt—and that's good for you, right? Stop trying to translate that which doesn't need words. Don't pick at my brain—

"Yo, you heard about Damien?"

I look up from the paper clenched between my fingertips.

It's Fizz, standing in front of my cell.

"Them dirty motherfuckers poked up Damien," he says, staring wide-eyed at the grout on the floor. "Can't believe this shit."

I slide my papers inside a manila envelope, drop them on my locker and stare at him. I got nothing to say. All I can do is blink. All I can do is forget Damien, erase the ghost of his presence from my memory. *Its* presence. It's already gone.

Fizz goes on: "Cocksuckers caught him in G-Block stairwell, coming from the bathhouse. Hit him wit' the bone crusher."

"Ice pick?"

"Yeah. Chest and throat."

"I knew that shit was coming," I say, then light a cigarette. Take a deep drag. Fizz leans against the wall. I hand him one and we smoke in silence. Keys jingle at the end of the tier, C.Os coming to lock someone up. To take him to the box and beat the black offa him. Right down to the white meat. To the bone. You ever had that kind of beating?

I doubt it.

I bump fists with Fizz, and he leaves to go lock in. In a minute or two, shit gonna get *real*. Real quick.

The C.Os bang their batons—I call them *clubs*—against everyone's bars and tell us to lock the fuck in. Guys grumble as they strut back to their cells then slam their gates closed as hard as they can. One of the rookie officers tries to make eye contact with me, to stare me down. I don't blame him. He don't know no better. All he know is what the other assholes tell him. They tell him what to feel, what to think. He looking for a sucker, someone to herb out, but he picked the wrong one today. He fresh out the academy, trying to earn his stripes. I meanmug him. Look him in the eye, introduce him to my world. Show him what fifteen joints up top look like.

The coward looks away.

Bitch ass.

I'm on my bunk blowing smoke rings when the thrashing begins. Not only can I hear everything, but I can *feel* the vibration against the thin metal wall as they wrestle with the prisoner inside the sardine-can of a cell.

When they come for you, they come for blood. They go hard. So you might as well get yours. Show them how you give it up.

The locker topples over. Something sounding like a radio smashes. Everybody yelling. Prisoners yelling. Officers yelling. It's going down. Punching. Kicking. Batons and walkie-talkies clatter on the floor. The guys are screaming now, shaking their bars. Some are screaming, "Fuck them up, son! Fuck them niggas up! Nigga, you better kill them motherfucking pigs!" And some are just screaming, letting off steam. Waking up the six realms of existence so they can share their pain with them. With the world. Don't matter if nobody hears, don't matter if nobody cares. Everybody just getting they shit off. Pigs and cons.

Regular prison shit.

Normal considering the environment. This zoo.

This concrete jungle full of snakes, lizards, rats, lions, and gorillas.

When they finally cuff the guy who killed Damien then drag him off the tier, I can tell his teeth been kicked in the way he moans, a trail of dark blood drooling outta the side his mouth. There's a puddle in front of my cell. Somebody gotta clean that shit up.

Guess who?

For the last three years, I been doing clean up duty around this shithole. Took me about six months of training—that's what they call it: *training*—to get certified, to use the chemicals, to use the right amount, to learn the proper procedure for disposal and blah blah blah blah. Anytime some shit go down and there bodily fluids around, I'm your man. Blue latex gloves and red caution bags. Powder and spray. Wait five to ten minutes, then wipe and mop. Pay is decent. Twenty bucks a pop.

Last week I had to clean the "shit room" (you don't need to do a bid to figure that one out) and the mental health ward upstairs. This fucking psycho, tree-jumping child molester sonofabitch slipped outta his turtle suit and smeared shit all over the observation window. All over. All. Over. Smiled at the officer while he did it. Heard he pulled a stunt to get there, slashed his wrists or something after getting extorted for his commissary by the hyenas. The usual.

You might think it's funny. Think you can't relate. But blood, shit, snot, piss, and semen ain't nothing to laugh about. You ever clean any of that shit in your life, you know what I'm saying.

I lay the powder down and wait a few seconds before spraying the cell floor. Spot a few teeth. I'll sweep those out later. The tier calmed down by now. Everyone chilled out, laughing, smoking. DutchMaster blunted and hoochie-poochied off bucket wine. The day's events already forgotten, lost in that hole of time, that point where the moment—before and after emptiness—ellipses and declines.

It's funny—well, not really—but in a lot of ways, I turned out just like my pops did. After all these years. Just like my moms said I would. Just like my teachers said I would. Sweeping and mopping floors. Cleaning up garbage. Making chump-change slaving for white people as a Maximum-A correctional facility janitor.

Surviving.

*Barely.*

Last I heard, pops was homeless. Wandering around Manhattan and looking for odd jobs. Prison really fucked him up. Big time. Hurt the whole family when he came home. Remember nights when, after getting dusted and drunk all night at the bar, he'd break in through the windows and start screaming at moms, screaming at us. That went on for a few years. Shit was fucked up. He was never the same. But then again, now that I think about it, after a few years in here, don't know if anyone is.

Found out yesterday why Damien got hit: a pair of Puma's. Yeah, you heard right, Puma's. Not Prada's. *Puma's.* A fucking pair of sneakers. How much a life is worth in this shithole. Kids these days is loco fo' real. I gotta get the hell outta here.

Lotta tension in the air today. Everybody on edge. Playing the wall real close. At this point in the game, one little incident, one little stupid word, one little stupid look could set off a colossal explosion of "razor-tag" and "hokey-pokey." Paranoia sets in. Guys become gladiators like it's the Olympics or some shit. And, if you in the yard, you expected to get down with the "Getdown." Get them before they get you. You might not wanna get involved, but dudes ain't trying to hear that, because if your peoples got beef with them, and they got beef with your peoples, they got beef with you, too. And that's a whole lotta beef you can't digest, just sitting there in the hollow of your gut—with no if-ands-or-buts between—and there nothing else you can do because anything after *but* is Bullshit.

Don't ask me why.

*Y* is a crooked letter.

You smell me?

Word on the street: Fizz and his peoples getting ready to approach them dudes with son who caught Damien slipping. Ready to put in some major work. I'm gonna fall back from the yard tonight, chill and read a book. Fizz ain't come around this morning. But that's outta respect; he know I ain't with the bullshit these days. I turn thirty-four next week. Got to grow up some-time, even if it's in a place where it's impossible to do so. Where whatever age you come in at, you stay at. That puts me at nineteen years old. A *ripe* nineteen years old.

The porter stops at my cell. He got cigarettes on the market. Newports. I tell him I'm good, I gotta couple pouches till next commissary. He mops the tier then comes back, looking vigilant. We shoot the shit a little bit.

Since after morning chow, people been real quiet. Too quiet. Rumors about administration locking this bitch down been spreading around faster than Zika. This ain't good.

"Lockdowns" mean bologna and cheese sandwiches, quarter waters, no commissary, no phone, no packages, and a whole lotta swamp ass for the next two weeks. And the worst part of it all: no cigarettes. Hope that don't happen, but if it does, it does. It is what it is.

Part of the experience.

About thirty or so minutes into evening rec, I hear shots go off in the guard tower. The sirens go off. I hear the C.O.s screaming, Get on the fucking ground! Put the goddamn knife down, asshole—right now!

I don't know why they even bother. Nobody ever listens. I mean, how can you? Put the knife down. For what? So I can get shanked in my fucking Adam's apple?

More shots go off.

I lay my book flat on my chest, close my eyes. It's gonna be a few hours before they get everyone back inside. Guess Fizz is gone. Going to the box. Or the infirmary. Or into town for an emergency hospital trip. This is like the eighth or ninth incident this week. And it's only Wednesday. I think about them Newports. Two weeks without menthol?

Sh*iiiii*t.

I quickly wave the porter over to my cell.

Whenever there a lockdown you can bet your pretty ass there gonna be a shakedown to go with it. "Shakedown" ain't no hip-hop dance. It means violation of every*thing* and every*one* for twenty-four hours. Losing property. Stripping down to your draws. Getting barked on, screamed at. The usual.

I got all my property—well, you really don't *own* nothing in here but that's what they call it to please the liberals and make them think our "rights" is being respected—laid out on my bed. Takes the joy from the pigs when they come to trash your shit. It been three days, so they should be coming to cause havoc real soon. If not today, then tomorrow.

The few things I care about, like my family photos and paperwork, is on the floor under the bed. Hopefully one of the lazy C.O.s search my cell. You luck out with one of them, and they don't fuck your shit up too much. If you quiet, polite. Carry yourself like a man. If you got time on your jacket, got an old number. They don't go as hard as they do with you as they do with the young boys, the gangbangers. But if you got any sexually-related crimes or any crimes involving children, you better pray to God or Lucifer or who-the-fuck-ever because whether you believe in any of that shit or not, you gonna get the kinda beating where people get all spiritual if and when they survive it.

Like POWs in Iraq, released in exchange for terrorists. You feel me? After situations like that, you see guys turn holier than thou. Start going to the church, the mosque, the synagogue. You ever see a black man with a yarmulke on?

No?

You will in here.

Trust me, I seen a lotta craziness on this bid, seen a lot of changes in dudes. But nobody takes the cake like my boy, Xavier. Can't *ever* forget that kid.

Xavier wasn't one them dudes that a place like this can change, he was one them dudes that changes places like this. Changes people. Kid came and flipped the whole culture on its head. If it wasn't for him, I never would've started writing. Never would've entered that contest and won first place. Never would've joined the poetry club at the library. And I know for a fact we wouldn't have no college in here either. Nobody ever challenged the Super-intendent about issues like that. Real issues. Shit that could actually benefit dudes, give them something positive to do with themselves. Keep them from killing each other. Nobody ever challenged the prison about anything, period. Ever. Nobody, except him. That's no bullshit I'm spitting.

Dudes still talk about him like he here. Kid sort of a legend. I gotta admit: I miss son.

The C.O.s is acting all rowdy downstairs on the first tier. I hear them banging they batons and yelling and acting stupid. These dumb rednecks have nothing better to do than get drunk, slap they wives and kids around, then come fuck with us like they live for this shit. Some of them do. Most of them just angry. Scared. Maybe a little bit of both, I don't know. About three months ago, somebody blasted one of the pigs across the face—buck-fiftied the poor motherfucker right outside the mess hall. Then they all settled down for a while. Now that everybody locked in? Hyped up like they got battery acid running through them or some shit. It cracks me up.

My thing is this: if you ain't really about that mess, stay in your lane and play your position. Don't front. Because, if you do, them wolves *will* come out.

The C.O.s is upstairs now, on the top tier.

My tier.

Here we go…

"Everybody down to their whites. You know the drill. And if you don't, your monkey ass better find out. Let's go, let's go," the sergeant yells, while nine or ten officers follow behind him, banging their batons against the bars. "Everybody standing, IDs on the gate. Face the back of the wall. When we tell you, slowly step away from the wall with your fingers interlocked behind your head. Any sudden movements and we take it is as a threat. Act accordingly."

A fat C.O, looking all Chris Farley in the face, stops in front of my cell. "Twelve cell," he yells to the officer at the control panel. My gate cracks.

"Step back, *slowly.*"

I step back.

"Turn around."

I turn around, glare at him.

"Drop the boxers."

I let them drop, show him what a real man looks like. Officer Beachball looks at my dick a few moments, then stares me in the eye. I can feel the racism radiating off his unibrow. I can tell we gonna have fun. A bead of sweat runs down his unshaved jaw.

"Lift your balls."

I lift them.

"Turn around. Spread them."

I turn around, spreading my cheeks so he can see what I had for breakfast. "C.O., I'm not due for a colonoscopy…for at least another six years," I say. My neighbor, watching his cell being searched, laughs. One of the C.O. laughs.

"Shut the fuck up. Get dressed."

I turn around and put my boxers on. Nostrils flaring, he watches while I dress. Looks me up and down. State greens from top to bottom, shower slippers, chip on my shoulder. The state property look.

"How long you been down?" he says.

"You should know," I say. "Look at my ID… you wanna join the fan club or something?"

"I'm not gonna ask you again, asswipe," he says, reaching for his baton. His comfort toy. "What's your number?"

*The year you was swimming in your daddy's nutsack, bitch.* "Longer than you been on the job."

Officer Beachball calls the sergeant. He need someone to hold his hand, I guess.

"What's the problem?"

"This guy's being an asshole," he says.

"Yeah, what he do?" the sergeant says, all rosy in the face.

"Jerkoff thinks he's too good to follow a direct order. Won't tell me his DIN, Sarge."

"You're calling me over for *this* bullshit… are you fucking kidding me?" he says before grabbing my ID off the gate. "It's right here. Right. Fucking. Here."

Officer Beachball glares at me.

"11-A-0671," the sergeant reads off the card. "That's you, right?"

"Yep," I say, struggling to keep a straight face. The sergeant belittles the officer, nods to me, then walks away. I enjoy the show. Sergeant known me for years. Know I don't start shit. Know I keep to myself. And don't mess with no one. Know I got fast hands, too.

All cops ain't bad, but all cops ain't good.

You feel me?

For the next forty-five minutes or so, I watch as the creep tosses and kicks everything in my cell, like a UPS box in a project hallway. He breaks everything that can be broke. I wanna choke him; I wanna throw him under the bed and kick a fucking field goal with his head, but I'm trying to change my life. I *need* to change. Fo' real. Need to stop smoking. Drinking. Cursing....

Well, maybe not the last thing.

But I'm really trying to be more of an example, like Xavier was for the young dudes. Kept a lotta them outta trouble. Till he left. Maybe I can do something good. Maybe I can be a pioneer of some movement in here. Something positive. Poetry club been falling off lately. Maybe it's up to me to continue what Xavier started. Keep dudes from killing each other. I don't know… I don't know what to do. I know something gotta happen, though.

Time to clean up, rearrange, and reorder things. My paperwork is fine. All over the cell—a couple sheets ripped up, a couple sheets in the toilet, but, other than that, I made out decent, pretty decent. Family photos unmolested. I'll put in a property claim for the cassette player and hotpot. Buy new ones while I wait for the claim to come through. Everybody on the block is gonna put one in, the way it looks around here. Motherfucking pigs destroyed *everything*.

Everything except heart.

And spirit.

Nah, they can't break that.

I remember this one time—don't know why I remember this, but—a few years back, when Xavier was my neighbor, we had this one crazy mother-fucking lockdown that lasted almost three weeks. Everybody was miserable. Place stunk worse than a bucket of chitterlings. Peep the funny part of the situation: this crazy son of a bitch, Xavier, flips out because we can't get no showers, so he decides to jam a toilet paper roll over his broom and light it up to set off the fire alarm. We all thought he lost it, thought he was smok-ing out everyone on the tier—till the alarm went off and the pigs had to emergency evacuate us to the yard.

Everybody went crazy.

That was when the superintendent got the call at his summer house. This Larry Byrd-looking sonofabitch was on the first thing smoking soon as he found out his employees was lazy, didn't wanna do shit beside sit on they fat ass and pretend to be running shit like normal. Flipped out when he found out how long they had us locked up for. Found out the families was calling the Governor's office for weeks. He really tore into the pigs when shit wound up in the *Post*—not because he cared, but because the blame fell on him. His administration. Superintendent got so mad he gave us extra privileges just to spite them pigs. Suspended half of them. Suspended with pay, of course. Gave us showers, phones, and visits every day. Soon as we got off lockdown, though, couple prisoners got jumped. Beat real bad. Bloodied up. Broken bones. The families kept calling and complaining, threatening to sue them and they future unborn generations if they didn't fall the fuck back. After that, things settled down for a while.

Pigs had no choice, really.

Me and Xavier got real tight a couple weeks later. Used to chef it up together and go halves on a blunt or a bottle of hooch. Talked for hours. Killed time. On weekdays, he'd make me read what he called *literature*. Novels mostly. I did a little writing, too. Poetry. Short stories. And after lights out, when everybody on the block was into some nonsense on the gate, son would send me book after book after book until my temples throbbed, and my eyes burned worse than the bulb next to my head, and I'd pass out with them damn books covering my face, like a bum on a park bench with his newspaper blanket tucked under his chin.

Like birds at rest, nesting over my dreams.

On the way to school he'd stop in front of my cell and laugh. I miss Xavier. Got his info. Heard he gotta book coming out... something about a writer who writes about writers. Funny dude. Might send him a line when I get out. That ain't gonna be for a few more years, but it's something to look forward to, I guess. Gotta have something, right?

"Montega got hit up, bro," says Chino to his neighbor on the way back from programs. "Grip up, my nigga, ya' heard. Shit might pop off tonight."

I walk by the two of them and fill my bucket up at the slopsink. I know Chino. The other guy new to the prison. Got here a couple weeks after the lockdown ended. Young. Dumb. Gangbanger. Probably got booted outta medium security being a knucklehead. Can't help but overhear the conversation as I add some soap powder to the water and stir it around. Watch the bubbles swirl into the vortex then pop. I add some more soap powder and head back to my cell. Kid still bugging out, yelling. Making a scene. I shake my head and sigh. Sometimes dudes get reckless. Make the environment real uncomfortable; can't control their emotions. Wrong people catch wind of it. Word spreads. Then bullshit starts.

"Them fucking prietos think they can style on any niggas they want, but shit ain't going down like that, Chino."

"Pisa, pisa, tranquiiiillo. Niggas might be listening mani. Breathe easy, we gonna handle that later. Let them sleep on us, for now—but be on point," says Chino.

"Nah, fuck that. Fuck that. I got my shit. Let's catch them now. Where they at? I hate them fucking pussies. What tier them niggas on? I don't give a fuck about no police, Chino. I don't give a fuck," the other guy says, pulling out a toothbrush with a thin piece of fiberglass on the side.

What he think this is… a barbershop? Hope whoever he got beef with don't bring a banger. A bonecrusher.

He gonna learn.

The hard way, by the looks of it.

I hear my neighbor laughing about something on the radio. Laughing with the madness of bliss experienced by those who suffer the most deeply. I do a little reading, wait for the C.O. to hand out the mail. He comes around. Stops at my cell. Flips through the stack, then keeps it moving.

Nothing for me.

Young kid in E-Block hung up this morning. Did it with his state blanket. Had to clean up the cell… after they wrapped him up in state sheets and threw out the body, like a sack of dirty laundry. Pine box if nobody claim him. It's tough this time of year.

Since I know how tonight gonna go, it's probably best I fall back from the yard and read a magazine or a book. Just chill and listen to my music. Been doing this a little while, seen this movie a million times. I know how it ends. Prison is like them *Star* magazines: same scene, different faces. Year in and year out. Ain't too much different than the freeworld. The real world. In some ways, the monsters in the town is more evil than the ones behind these walls. Think about it.

Hold that down.

Nothing shocks me anymore. I laugh at them crazy bastards in Times Square screaming about "end times." World ain't getting worse: it *always* been fucked up. We still got nukes, financial ruin, corrupt governments, rape, robbery, disease, flooding, earthquakes, starvation, riots, looting, genocide, and anarchy. Nothing new. Sons still killing fathers; daughters still dumping babies down garbage chutes. People still overdosing and jumping off bridges like the shit in style. It ain't the new normal, it's the old one. And it ain't going nowhere anytime soon. So don't get it twisted.

Went to the mental health ward today. Cleaned up some shit and piss. Little bit of vomit. Semen. The usual. Saw my boy, Craig, in the infirmary. Told me Fizz got two years in the box. And a few new charges to go with it:

Weapons. First-degree assault. Attempted murder. The works.

Hopefully, he won't spend the rest of his life behind bars. Some dudes gotta learn the hard way, though. It is what it is. I tried to work with the kid.

Can't change people if they don't wanna change.

People change when they get tired of the bullshit.

That's what Xavier would say if he was here. But he ain't. And he ain't coming back, neither. That's a good thing. I'm proud of him, fo' real. Now it's my turn.

Whenever I need inspiration, I read one of the things he wrote, one of the things he left behind—said caused him too much pain to take with him—and I think. I just sit on my bunk and think. Like meditation. You ever do that?

Sometimes, while sitting on my bunk and staring at the bars in front of me, I imagine him here, his mirror hanging out the bars, teaching me how to read. He gave me my first book a few Christmases ago: *Thus Spoke Zarathustra*. My first Christmas present ever. Shit, my first-ever Christmas. Last one, too. Nobody celebrate holidays in here.

Ain't shit to celebrate.

Just another day.

I wanna write something great. I wanna say something great. I wanna get outta my head. I wanna empty it all out. Feel free. Weed and alcohol can only do so much for someone, you know? Some*one*. That's all I am. One man. Maybe not even that.

While waiting to go to commissary a couple days ago, some young dude with a fresh DIN started drilling me with questions, asking me how I was doing and all this other dumb shit, trying to be funny for his peoples, so I spazzed out:

"You think this shit a game, kid? You know what it's like to lose everything and everyone? You stupid or crazy? Ain't nobody laughing with you, they laughing at you. You still a kid. This life ain't for you, homeboy. You don't know pain. Think you do, you don't. You wanna talk to me, get to know me, you better be willing to share the burden. Why you asking how I'm doing? I look like I'm doing good? I'm in fucking prison, stupid. Anyone here look like they doing good? What you asking me questions for anyway? What you gonna do? You gonna help *me*? If you can't do that, then don't ask me shit. You don't know me, kid. Ask one of these dudes around here if you wanna learn the ropes, want someone to hold your hand. Don't ask me nothing. Don't ask me shit. And don't…don't ask me my name. Nobody asks me my name. I don't have one. State took that away a long time ago. Took that when they took my pops. You hear me? Look at me when I'm talking to you. Yeah, look me in the eye. All that's left is me. *Me*. A man with his word and his honor. A man. That's all I am. An ungodly godlike man. You don't know what that means. Might never. Now get your shit together, and stop being a fucking clown before somebody really hurts you."

*An ungodly godlike man.* Don't know what that last thing meant, don't know where it came from, but I said it. And I meant it. Guess Xavier's presence still here.

Anyway, the young dude looks at me strange. Shuts his mouth. Keeps it moving. Everyone quiet. Whole vibe changed.

That's how I like it. That's how you gotta be with most people in here. Let them know you ain't playing no games, that you ain't the one. Gotta keep your circle small in here. In the freeworld, too. The only way to avoid the bullshit.

Craig came by later and talked to me. Smoked a Swisher. Told me to go easy on the kid. Told me he fresh up top. I was like him once. Ain't know how serious shit was. Came in the system with my head up my ass. I'll see what the kid about. Give it some time. Maybe talk to him in the yard. See if he join a gang or get into some nonsense before inviting him to poetry club. I'll work with him.

Everybody deserves a chance.

Later that night, when I got back to my cell after programs, I found one of Xavier's monologues crumbled up behind my locker. Dusty and waterlogged. Must have been there since the shakedown. I read it out loud, although I got it memorized. Got it on cap. With a pen in my hand and composition notebook on my bed, I read it to my neighbor—Xavier's spirit nodding in approval—before ripping it up:

Stop trying to translate that which doesn't need words. Don't pick at my brain.

You probably think I'm an arrogant prick for coloring this transmission with such flowery language and you'd be right to do so. Perfectly right. It's understandable; I know you hate me deep down in your soul. Soul. What the hell does a soul have to do with anything? Oops! There I go again. I said *hell* just now, didn't I? See what I mean, it's embedded in me. I find it very amusing.

Ha, Ha. Ha. Ha, Ha.

But back to what I was saying:

Remaining a sheep won't help you in this world. While you're out there—grazing, mindlessly minding your own business—packs of ravenous wolves are salivating at the mouth, waiting for you to venture out the pasture, out the loving eye of the Sheppard who cares for you (as long as he can shear your coat for spiritual profit). But with no wind, the shadow of this monolith stays glued in place, like a fateful stain, a telltale mark clinging to the earth as it goes around and around the sun for another millennia to come. Never ending. Ever.

Some will frolic in its dream; some will slash through its illusion. But the system remains. There will always be fools. Victims. This is the cold, hard reality of the world. Kill or be killed. So be a lamb why don't you?

I'm joking.

I would never wish such an abominable fate on you. Or anyone. What kind of monster do you take me for? And yes, I apologize in advance for my use of the word *fate*. Who am I to condemn? I am not God ...

So, then, you ask, who am *I*? A sage, a prophet, a demon? A raving lunatic, perhaps? You wish to understand me, my mode of thinking. But how can you ever hope to understand me and my teachings when you don't understand your*self*?

Ha. Ha, Ha, Ha. Ha.

Who are *you*?

That is the real question.

Like that which is not thought by the mind, but by which the mind thinks, you will always be a step behind. Many steps behind. But there's a solution to all of this, my friend: You must slay the master. Me, *I*.

Become the master. Seize life by the throat and take control.

Kill your idols.

*Third Place*

# My Penal Vacation
## JOHN CEPHAS YOUNG

"How are you, this morning?"

"Oh, just great, Thanks for asking," I respond to the Middle-Eastern man lurking in his doorway as I journey down the hall. One thing is clear, neither of us gives a damn how the other is doing. This is just something we do: a sort of predatorial ritualistic dance we perform at 5:30 am. It started about two weeks ago, when I moved in with my girlfriend down the hall.

While it's rather unfortunate, the truth is—as a fairly dark black man at 6'3" and 230 pounds—I've grown accustomed to this kind of lurking, "watch him" behavior. It's an immutable part of my existence. So I live with it. Outside the apartment building, the residual rain litters the ground, the sky is grayish-blue, and the faint aroma of coffee and cigarettes lingers in the air. And while the average person would not automatically associate these smells with anything ceremonious, I smell freedom; a whole 87 days of it. Yes, compared to the stench of mens' feet and suppressed farts that I was forced to inhale in prison, this is paradise to my nose, even if it just says Summerset Apartments across the building.

On the street, light clusters of patriots, scattered along the sidewalk, are starting their day. Unlike prison, where we all started our day with a somber walk to the chow-hall, here everybody's busy with their own distinctive act of readying themselves; like the father trotting toward the idling van, double-parked in front of his building. He joins his family waiting inside, and off they go. He waves to me as he passes by (another fast-forming ritual). Or the rotund Asian woman waiting for the approaching school bus with her two kids, the giant tires on the yellow bus wrestles and dishevels tiny water droplet as it passes.

Then there's the white kid with the long denim shorts, with an even longer wallet chain dangling along his leg. His spikey greased hair, and black leather choke-chain, featuring shiney spikes, manages to sparkle somehow as he zooms past. Obviously, dress code is not a concern in his line of work, assuming that's where he's off to this morning.

I get to the bus stop, directly across the donut shop, and sit atop the backrest on account of the wet bench. I used to go into the little shop for coffee every morning, till I caught myself unconsciously casing the joint: post traumatic-stress from doing a sixteen-year bid. Whenever I walk into a business establishment, I automatically start searching for cameras, the closest exit, number of employees, etc.

After concluding that the coffee shop had no surveillance cameras, two elderly employees, booming business on account of the college down the street, and a back exit that led into an alley, I decided to skip my morning coffee.

I caught the elderly lady looking toward the bus stop a few times, probably disappointed at the loss of a customer. Count your blessings lady, I think to myself. This is one customer you're better off without.

Frankly, it's mind-boggling how just three months ago I was confined to segregated housing, deemed a threat to the general population in prison, cautiously handcuffed through the tray-slot, and escorted by two correctional officers everytime I came out of my cell. That was until my release date. As if, according to their "expert prognosis," at exactly 4:00 am, May 7, 2014, I became sane enough to push back into society.

Now, I'm not complaining—I love my freedom—I'm merely pointing out that being in an extremely hazardous environment, like prison, for 5,740 days, then thrust into the total opposite within minutes, creates a great deal of mental shock. I don't think you need to be a psychologist to figure that one out.

Eventually, I spot the green Honda amid the morning traffic. The driver's name is Jamal, and we work together. Actually, he's the reason I even got the job. He's also my girlfriend's older brother. The only problem is that on any given day, he'll simply decide to skip work, schedule be damned! So the day I miss the bus waiting for him could easily be the day he decides to stay home. It's happened twice. I need this job. If the bus comes before him, that's how I get to work.

My first gig out of prison was at an oil refinery, where they strap a paper-mask over your face—theoretically, this is to filter at the toxic fumes, but that's like trying to clear a flood with a spoon—fasten a harness to your mid-section, and drop you down an oil well. Most people vomit as soon as they're pulled up; eleven people die a year. One day was enough for me. It's a shame that nobody has a decent job for an ex-con. If anything, you'd think they'd offer some kind of incentive to employers that help reintegrate a guy into society, that's if they wanted to reduce crime. But what do I know?

"Naw, I ain't think that," I lie and quickly get into the car. Jamal's a big fellow—mostly fat—with a gleaming bald spot and a Hitler mustache. He smokes like a chimney: Newports during work hours, and God-knows-what off the clock.

"You ain't hurd wha' happened last night?," he inquires as he merges back into traffic. Now, Jamal is the biggest liar I've met in my life: another reason I'd rather catch the bus sometimes. I mean, district attorneys could take lessons from this guy on how to fabricate bullshit stories. "Ah man, so I was at the...," at this point, I tuned him out. See, Jamal's one of these guys that's obsessed with creating the bad boy image for himself. He wants to be seen as hard convict-thug, but he wouldn't bust a grape in a fruit fight.

There's nothing glorious about a lengthy criminal record and having to pee in a cup for a parole officer. But I suspect that's the main reason he hangs with me, to come off as some sort of thug or gangster. That's also why all of his over-embellished stories end with him either pistol-whipping somebody, or telling somebody to "shut the fuck up!" There's also the occasional "You-must-not-know-who-you-messing-with, Nigga, I'm J-Bone" endings. (I never heard anybody call him J-Bone, mind you.)

He claims we knew each other eighteen years ago, before my prison bid. I'm almost certain that too is a lie. I mean after being tried as an adult at sixteen, being the youngest inmate on a Level 4, 180 Yard, where I mastered the art of stabbing my fellow inmates with prison shanks that I stashed up my rectum, who could blame me for forgetting an eighteen-year-old friendship that never existed in the first place?

I remember on my release date looking in all four directions and thinking, it really didn't matter which direction I wandered off. Since the death of my mother while I was locked up, I have nothing anchoring me to any location on this planet.

The wonderful Department of Corrections handed me $200, $80 of which they immediately snatched back for a mandatory ride in a van to the closest bus station. The driver warns you to stay inside the Greyhound station, as the town does not want your kind lingering around.

Thus, forty-five minutes after being caged in a 10x16 cell for a little short of two decades, I was standing at a bus station feeling out of place. Out the window, the cars looked too big. Inside, everybody was moving and talking at once, and total strangers kept walking behind me. I bolted into a bathroom stall, where I stayed for close to an hour. Finally, I purchased a ticket to the San Fernando Valley because...well...that's the last area I was at before my arrest. I guess home is where you once were. From the bus station in Van Nuys, I found the GR office. I made it to the office before 1:00 but quickly learned that my conviction made me ineligible for general relief (a measly $220).

I did, however, qualify for emergency food stamps ($80 worth) and a two-week voucher at a roach-motel in the heart of downtown Los Angeles. I spent my first night out of prison scrubbing mildew at the bottom of the shower, smelling wrack through the vents, and trying to remember the last time I had a tetanus shots.

"So then I said shut the fuck up bitch 'fore I pistol-whip that ass, must not know who you talking too, Nigga, I'm J-Bone. J-Bone, mutherfucker!"

"Is that right?," I murmur, recognizing the end of yet another episode of "Jamal and the fairy tales!" Oddly enough, all his stories share the odd commonality of ending exactly when we reach the job site. No matter what audacious adventure the great J-Bone goes on, he always gets the girl and walks off into the sunset right when we get to the job site. If there's traffic that day, the adventure is more daring.

The construction site is in a gated community. It's several blocks of condominiums in various stages of construction. Wooden framed condos lines both sides of the bare streets, and groups of constructions workers are gathered in front at various spots.

Our work area is at the very back corner of this new community. Three giant pickup trucks mark our specific location for the day. He parks by the trucks, and we exit the vehicle. The foreman is smoking a cigarette by one of the trucks. He signals us over then glances at his watch. He's a bald-headed white man with tattoos. I had difficulty working with him at first. For sixteen years, I'd been warring with white boys in prison. And no, not warring in the metaphorical sense. I mean literally engaged in brutal brawls on the yard while the guards emptied out their M-16s at us. The officers were mostly whites; guess who they were aiming at? I've been stabbed nine times, and been hit with more rubber bullets than I care to remember. I haven't as much as shared a smile with a white man in sixteen years. Next thing I know, I'm working for one.

"I'm good, just ready to work."

"Good to hear," he responds, emphatically, shaking my hand and patting me on my shoulder. For a split second, I feel the urge to clock him across the jaw. This is just too much contact for me. I give that feeling a second to pass. "Jamal, you're working with Jose today." To me, he says, "I got something different for you today." He leads me around an unfinished condo.Several workers are hammering a giant frame where a door will soon be erected. A boom-box fills the air with an accordion and harmonica-driven mariachi. And despite the language barrier, the singer's somber baritone has its desired effect deep within my loins.

We stop at the back corner of the facility. In front of us is a steep hill with several deep gutters dug across the surface. I'm not exactly sure what we're looking at, till he points to the hard plastic pipes wedged inside the grooves. "They laid the plumbing a couple days ago. I need you to cover the pipes back up, they'll probably grow some grass over it at some point." Now,

I'm not a mathematician, mind you, but the incline on this mount is easily about 70-75 degrees. In other words, it's so steep that none of the dirt they dug up stayed on the hill.

It all gathered at the foot of Mount Kilimanjaro. He must've sensed my hesitation—I wasn't putting much effort into hiding it—because, finally, he said, "There's a rope tied to that tree up there. Get it around your waist. It'll help you maintain footing. There's a pile of dirt over there." I simply nod in response. He pats me on the shoulder again before leaving me to my assignment. I exhale deeply, then go over to the dirt pile. After grabbing the shovel stuck in the middle, I reappraise the hill. My initial challenge is hiking up Mount Everest to the rope, then back down to the pile of dirt. Then back up to the highest gutter, balancing a shovel of sand.

I start my ascent to the tree of life atop the incline, thinking if God had just stuck the forbidden tree atop this great mount, humanity wouldn't be cursed like this.

On the fourth step, mud sticks to the bottom of my hand-me-down boots as I slide back down. That's when I'm slapped with the realization that there's no way to climb this thing without using my hands. So, I lower myself, and proceed to crawl on all fours, thinking about all those classes I took in prison, as mud sticks to my fingers. I earned a bachelor's degree in liberal arts and became a certified paralegal. I bought into the happy endings, the fairy tales. I really believed society would let me back in. You know, forgive my wrongs and allow me to move on. What an idiot was I?

A convict's debt to society is never paid. I remember a story I read in the LA Times about cleaning up Downtown. When identifying the scum of society, the writer named prostitutes, pimps, drug addicts, and felons on parole. I let that thought linger in my mind as I tie the wet rope around my waist. I seriously consider just sitting on my ass and sliding down. Why not? Drug addicts and felons, huh?

After washing up with the water hose while the other workers smiled and snickered, I approached the lunch truck that was idling on the dirt road. This, too, is rapidly becoming a routine. Of all the construction workers surrounding the lunch truck, Jamal is the only black. The fact is, I simply don't trust him enough to have my back in case they attack. I try to tell my brain: Relax! This isn't prison, Nobody's looking to attack you. But it's not that simple.

For the past sixteen years, I haven't approached one white man without backup. That isn't something that just goes away when you remove the fence and gun towers. So instead, I stand here starving as the delicious aroma of grilled onions and carne asada fills the air.

"You straight?" Jamal asks, approaching me through the crowd without a care in the world. "You ain't want nothing?", he adds while trying to squeeze the whole burrito into his mouth. And I think, man, ignorance is bliss. "Could you get me something? I got the money right here."

"Man, I don't understand how come you can't get it" he manages to piece together around a mouthful of hot burrito. "Come on, J-Bone, help a brother out." With his ego inflated, he motions for the money. I dig into my pocket, pull out a ten-dollar bill, and slap it into his palm. And off he goes, through the boisterous crowd, on a mission to secure my lunch.

At three o'clock, half the gutters are filled. I'm balancing a shovel-load, the scorching sun dispelling rivulets of sweat down my forehead and back, and wondering if the oil refinery will take me back.

I'm within seconds of dropping the shovel, sliding down this hill and telling the foreman to kiss my ass, when he shows up and switches my position for the day. I'm to deliver piles of freshly cut 2x4's to different sites, as needed. I fold up my shirt, place it on my shoulder, and get to carrying.

At 5:00, we finish for the day. Jamal's grinning by the car when I get there. My arms and shoulder are covered in splinters, there's mud all over my boots and pants, and I smell like a freakin' Greek gymnasium. I'm asleep before we leave the lot.

"A, yo, Darian! Darian!," Jamal's voice interrupts my sleep. I look around and realize we're a block from my girl's apartment. "Man, drop me off right there," I say, indicating the liquor store on the right.

"You need something?," he asks as he turns into the parking lot. "I'ma wait out there," he adds.

"Naw, you straight."

"You sure?"

"Yeah," I say, slam the door and go into the liquor store. Inside the store, I approach the counter and purchase a stick of gum. Out the corner of my eyes, I see Jamal pull out the lot and I sigh in relief. "You okay?, you look tired," the lady at the counter observes. "I'm fine," I murmur and exit the store.

The truth is, I have no interest in chewing gum right now. I've just learned to keep my business concealed. My girlfriend is on Section 8 - where the government pays her rent, as long as she does not allow any felons to stay with her. You know, no scum-of-the-earth types. She lets me sleep there at night, reasoning that the Section 8 office shouldn't send an inspector to her apartment at night.

In the four years she'd lived there nobody'd come by to inspect, until I moved in. I'm almost certain it's the same middle-eastern man in the hallway this morning that's reporting us. He's the building manager. I don't know what I would do if my actions rendered my girlfriend and her four-year-old daughter homeless. So, for the second time today, I sit at a bus stop and contemplate my life: a fierce battle between my ambitions and my reality, my goals and society's impediments. When the bus comes, I climb aboard, tired and covered in mud.

There's no empty seats, so I hang onto a rail and try not to get tossed around too bad. A few blocks later, a seat becomes available. I collapse into it and pretend not to notice the guy next to me inching away. Who could blame him? A few stops later, I get off the bus. I'm practically wrestling my equilibrium when I enter the gym. It took awhile for me to find a place to wash up without getting arrested. Using my girlfriend's credit card, I signed up a week ago and incorporated this into my daily routine.

To keep from looking like a bum, I sit at the universal weight machine for a while. The plan is to work out, then go into the locker room for a shower, and change into fresh clothes—except the boots, I need those for tomorrow—then, basically, meander through the streets till a safe time to go to the apartment. But as I sit at the machine, I'm just too tired to even pretend-work-out.

So I stare at the machine, then at my sordid pants and boots. Abruptly, I get up and head toward the showers. I glance at the people eagerly exercising—several pedaling away on stationary bikes—and I think of prison. Except there we worked-out-for survival. There, with all of life's luxuries stripped away, men are reduced to their most primitive: the survival of the fittest. Literally, the strongest survive: the alpha males. You did everything in your power to get strong. Your life could depend on it.

After my shower, I head to the bus stop to sit for a while. Around 7:30, I catch the bus and head home. It's a little earlier than we agreed, but I'm tired. Monday down, five more days to go.

Day 96; almost made it to 100. I don't know if I should be disappointed or proud of myself for surviving as long as I did; Surviving in this strange, unforgiven and desolate terrain.

"Baby, what happen? Don't worry I'ma drive behind y'all to the station." My girlfriend's screams reaches me in the back of the police car. We're in the parking lot of the donut shop.

I want to tell her not to bother—that I'm only going back home. But I don't. Instead, I just stare at the little donut shop and breathe deeply. Finally, the officer gets in the car and drives off. The hard plastic seat digs into my back; tears blur my vision as we turn onto the main street. Prison has ruined me. Unbeknownst to even me, they've reprogrammed my brain; reconditioned me into a monster. A dangerous half-witted beast, barely able to function in their society. Ill-equipped to operate their smartphones and skinny computers.

The word convict stenciled across my forehead. My scarlet letter. A label that encourages employers to tip their noses at me. A label that motivated the police to stop, search, and mistreat me, that made my need for assistance a laughing matter at the county office. It's like the judge's gavel at my sentencing permanently hammered me into the lower bracket of society. At the red light, I recall my job in prison as a law library clerk. There, other inmates sought my guidance; they venerated my wit. Later—while earning my paralegal certification—I became the inmates' representative. The one that relayed the warden's desires to the inmates.

Armed with a folder and a clipboard, I was genuinely respected. For a few seconds, I wonder if it's better to be a big fish in a small, shallow, pond, or a starving guppy barely alive in the vast and salty Atlantic Ocean. Is it realistic to expect a guy not to get money the only way he knows how while all other avenues are being maliciously closed off to him? Would it be rational for such a person to feel like his failures are his own fault, since he's purposely overlooking his skills? Would such a person, at the very least, need some sort of psychological assistance to reacclimate himself into society?

I think about the inspector from Section 8 standing in the doorway at 1:00am (I guess, we were wrong) then, me helping my girl and her daughter pack their things, unable to look into her eyes, my shame, palpable and thick, suffocating me. Then I recalled bursting into the donut shop, feeling more like a victim than ever. Who locks an emergency exit? That is illegal, a safety hazard. I guess, so am I.

I let the familiar cuffs dig into my flesh and enjoy the ride back to prison, home sweet home. Or better yet, home is where you once were.

# ESSAY

*First Place*

# The Swallow War
## SAINT JAMES HARRIS WOOD

After fifteen years down, I assume that prison life can't get any more off-kilter or annoying; but then, some cruel functionary starts a war against the local swallows. Each early dawn and during the fading light of dusk I love to watch the hardy little birds hurtling in tandem by the hundreds, coasting and whipping around the sky, exercising or herding bugs maybe, or perhaps just flying for the joy of it. I enjoy it, watching their huge swarm, a thousand strong, wheeling around like drunken feathered acrobats, breathtaking and beautiful as they pursue and eradicate every bee, fly, mosquito, moth and whatever else is in the air and smaller than the hungry little assassins. Watching the sparrows is better than tv or pinochle and has the distinct bouquet of freedom.

In the hills surrounding my home, the California Men's Colony, dwell macabre flying spiders who contrive to get to the top of our absurdly high (50 yards) light towers. The ambitious spiders lay thousands of eggs up there, and when the babies hatch, windy days are a signal for them to make web kites, and all at once the entire spider congregation takes off, mostly to be killed and eaten by the swallows, thank God; but last year the flying baby spiders launched themselves while the sparrows were off somewhere else, having heard of special mud for their nests in another county. The spiders spread across the sky, the yard, all over the buildings and grass, landing on our clothes and hair for an hour, until finally the sparrows returned home. It was a scene, or more properly an outburst of nature (a tantrum?) to see a thousand swallows dodging about en masse, performing maneuvers, eradicating the remaining spiders, still aloft. The baby spiders take it stoically as a countless number of their comrades had made it to the ground before the massacre. Like everyone, I can't help but wonder how the swallows manage to perform their complicated mass dance and aerial gyrations—spinning, swirling, churning, clouds of feathers and grace so unlike our clumsy human world—without ever crashing into each other and falling to the ground like Icarus, or me.

These American Cliff Swallows have been coming to San Luis Obispo for a thousand years, flying up from Goya, Argentina (if we are to believe them), and once here they frantically, industriously search out little globs of mud and build nests that resemble tiny brown desert igloos. The prison is smack dab in the middle of the little birds' centuries old customary nesting grounds. Figuring that we've placed the prison here for their convenience the swallows build their nests in the infrastructure of the steel girders—imagine a bridge built in a square with all the little caches, tiny lairs, and small dens that three stories of steel beams offer. This singular edifice sits in the center of the prison; it's open air and we call it the plaza. There are a couple of trees, some sickly grass and a 100 yard circular sidewalk in the plaza connecting our four yards. All the cops, free staff and convicts (around 3,000 people) march through it to work, to school, to the library and everywhere else we are compelled to go during the day, from four in the morning until around ten at night. Right above the sidewalk is the metal structure with its niches, nooks and crannies—about every four-five inches—where the swallows build their nests, and there are a couple thousand of these spaces in the plaza. It is a wonderfully odd and happenstance open air aviary—except of course for the barbed wire and incarceration. The swallows are free and the humans are trapped. As we walk back and forth beneath their nests to school and work, the swallows, who apparently aren't afraid of humans, stare grumpily at us, trespassing in their prison.

For nine years I've watched the whole process: birds arrive, build nests like tiny lunatic construction crews, at dawn and dusk they twirl and swirl through the sky (often feinting and mock fighting for obscure reasons), and conveniently patrol our little valley and eat countless bugs. Out here in the near wilderness there are bugs galore and I am grateful that the mosquitoes, midges and spiders are dealt such a blow, the swallows keeping them from my flesh. They have to maintain their high pitched metabolisms, fuel up for all the precise turbulent aerial displays, and when the time comes, feed their fledglings. Eggs are laid and the mock fighting increases as they defend their nests from imaginary threats. Soon (two weeks), frighteningly tiny swallows are hatched, mindlessly cheeping for bugs and whatever else is on the menu. In quick order the fledglings are stumbling around, careless of danger (the hideous local seagulls sometimes eat them); with typical swallow speed the kids are as big as their parents within a month. The fledglings and their parents fly around for three months or so, dealing further blows to the neighborhood bug population; and then, like a theatrical troupe, the swallows leave town—the whole mad swarm wheel in circles putting on one last show with the rising sun, then it is back to South America or Jerusalem (a tale that has drifted up the coast from San Juan Capistrano) or wherever. It is all rumor to me, we're not allowed the Internet. One of my friends googled swallows and ended up garnishing the Jerusalem myth with the implausibly tall, probable fairy tale that the swallows carry twigs while flying over the Atlantic towards Israel, so that they can occasionally lay their twig in the ocean and settle down on it to float for a while and catch some zzzs. The remarkable little birds even have exceptional fables—likely by-products of their extensive wandering.

But then, suddenly, some deranged prison bureaucrat decides to destroy the nests, and covers the infrastructure with nets, thinking to stop the swallows' cycle so that they will go elsewhere. The plan fails completely. The swallows are outraged and flip out for an entire day. Since they seem quite mad to start with, it is sad and disturbing to see them lose it. In a rage, the swallows swarm that night like usual, taking out their fury on the bugs, but the fluidity and poetry is gone, and though they still somehow avoid mid-air crashes—their usual nighttime display of flying beauty is gory and tumultuous, organized chaos the order of the day, all elegance vitiated. Where the swallows all previously stuck together in a flock during their evening acrobatics, now dozens of them fly off madly, helter skelter, nearly (but never) running into buildings and even people. I was worried: for the birds, for the eggs that had no place to be laid, for nature itself. Watching cops bring in crews to destroy the remaining nests and put up the nets is aggravating, and I try to find an address for The National Swallow Association or somesuch. Swallows in California have had problems with humans before. Near the end of the 1800's the tiny colorful feathers on the Barn Swallow's rumps were put on hats desired by politicians' wives and prostitutes. Hatters had the swallows killed, plucked the feathers, and threw away the remains. Subsequently, almost driving the Barn Swallow into extinction, in the name of fashion. This threat led to the founding of the first Audubon Society in 1888.

I don't go near the plaza for a long weekend. On Monday, walking to school, I see that the instinct-driven little savages have built new nests (the previous nests had taken at least a week to build) everywhere, including some hanging off the nets like an illusion—Daliesque constructs in weird new shapes, many of them twice as big as their previous nests. There are mud nests in light fixtures, on trash cans, on clocks, on top of other nests! The little bastards refuse to yield or surrender. I don't think swallows know how to give up. The dauntless creatures have to deal with hurricanes, hungry hawks, foxes, and every other kind of test nature can throw at them—humans probably just seem like incompetent skinny bears on a rampage, to be ignored. It's not over yet, it is time to lay eggs, a dishearteningly dramatic development. If the prison wants to attack nature I don't know why the cops don't start with the cursed seagulls who are here year-round shitting on everything (and everyone!) in huge amounts with wild abandon, while fighting insanely over garbage and squawking obnoxiously like aging hookers. Seagulls will lock beaks over an apple core until they're bleeding. Everybody hates the seagulls. So, if the authorities want to deal with a bird problem, they should deport the goddamn witless seagulls back to the sea.

Strangely, there appear to be twice as many nests and swallows as there were before the attempted eviction. In the past, other than giving us grumpy looks with their beady eyes, the swallows ignored people. They mostly won't even take food from us (while the seagulls wait outside the chow hall and beg like retarded dogs). I get the impression that the swallows are now riled and keeping an eye on us. Luckily, the cops have given up after the first round of smashed nests. And nobody knows who ordered it. As most of the happenings at the California Men's Colony, it is a mystery. Nevertheless, this year's swallows are laying their eggs, and things have returned to what passes for normal.

*Second Place*

# Going Forward with Gus
## STERLING CUNIO

Over a dying man stands another who has committed murder. The dying man speaks of his kids and of seeing angels. He talks in between bouts of choking on his own blood as the tumor in his throat hemorrhages. The other man nods silently. There will be no help for the dying man as the cancer consumes him. There will be no help for the other as he serves life without parole. Both will die in prison: One will be dead within days; the other when his sentence ends.

The two men cry and pray on the top floor infirmary of the Oregon State Penitentiary in Salem. Although situated in the middle of the state's capital city, the 2000 men who live, work and die behind thirty-foot walls are invisible. In a hall off the main ward there are two rooms reserved for hospice, where men too weak to stand on their own or breathe without machines await death. Prisoners serving as hospice volunteers are their final earthly companions.

His name is Gus. He is a 63-year old father of six and grandfather of thirteen. He's been in prison for two years. He prides himself on the fact he worked his entire life and is leaving this world owing nobody. He is proud that his children are good parents. He played baseball for thirty-years, worked as a chef and drove long-haul trucks across America. When he wasn't working, he was fishing or playing in the park with the grandkids. He had strength then—he could walk, run, and play then. That was before a six-year battle with melanoma left him bed-ridden, weighing less than 100 pounds and struggling to breathe through an airway restricted by a throat tumor that was suffocating him.

I am the lifer standing over Gus in the final moments. Like him, I am expected to die in prison. Unlike him, I'll have spent most my life in prison, sentenced to de facto life without parole at the age of sixteen. The Centers for Disease Control has established that life spans for prisoners are significantly shorter than the national average. Life expectancy for inmates is 50.1 years, according to the Oregon Department of Corrections Government Efficiencies and Communications Office. If my life conforms to the statistical norm, I will die here after having served 34.5 years for my responsibility in the murder of two people. I have, statistically, 13.6 more years to live.

When I was twelve years old I was orphaned to the streets after my grandmother, the superwoman that raised me, died suddenly. After bouncing around the country to the homes of different relatives who either couldn't or didn't want to care for me, and living like a runaway, I became involved in the culture of street crime. Seeking to enhance status and solidify inclusion among a group of peers fascinated with gangster archetypes and criminal lifestyles, I and another teenager kidnapped and shot a young couple. It happened right down the road from the prison where I now write this. In 1994, when I was sixteen years old, I shattered people's lives before I understood the value of life, and it has haunted me ever since.

Gus's cancer spread first by attaching itself to his jaw; the doctors had to cut out so much of the bone to remove it that what remained of his jaw broke and caused him to slur when he spoke. He managed to speak anyway, and whenever he talked to me about separation from family or facing death he would advise, "Don't dwell on the negative—it only invites woe." It was an astonishingly positive message from a man dying in prison, but his words didn't begin to relieve the personal guilt I carry. Extinguishing life through violence is an irreparable act. My soul aches, and the only shaky solace I can seek is found in acts of service. There is no lasting relief. Guilt never allows those who accept responsibility for irreparable acts to move on. Yet, hope for spiritual redemption compels me to go forward in search of personal purpose through small acts of kindness. Fortunately, kindness is a choice and opportunities to practice it are abundant. Even in prison.

Because Oregon does not release the terminally ill, many die serving their sentences, separated from friends and family. For this reason some prisons operate hospices within their walls. Oregon was one of the first, but now there are more than 75 in-prison hospices, 50 percent of which depend on prisoners as volunteers. I was one of the few people fortunate enough to be selected as a volunteer in the OSP hospice program developed in 1999 by prison administrators, medical staff, chaplains, and fellow convicts and based on the idea that even those in prison should not die alone. Twenty volunteers selected from within the prison were trained for ninety hours by medical professionals and institutional counselors to provide support to others at the end of life. The prisoners are trained in concepts of death and dying; interpersonal communication; bereavement; understanding diseases and conditions; handling patients; hospice care; and comfort measures.

Death has been one of the primary forces to shape the course of my life, and loss—both incidental and intentional—has been a constant. When I began attending hospice meetings in 2014, I felt conflicted, reluctant, and fearful of bonding intimately with someone who would soon be gone. But all of that changed after I sat through my first vigil. When the medical staff determines that death is imminent, the patient is placed on a vigil and accompanied by volunteers around the clock. Ideally, those scheduled for vigil have already had a strong connection with the patient. However, a mistake by a new officer and a new nurse thrust me into the heart of hospice when they sent for me instead of a fully trained volunteer.

It was in late June of 2015 when two officers appeared at my cell door. "Cunio, get ready," one of them said. "Ready for what?" I asked, with rising dread. In the past, the sudden appearance of officers at my door in the middle of the night generally meant beatings while being dragged off to "the hole," where I spent much of my first decade of imprisonment. Those who stay there long term, as I did throughout most my twenties, develop a "me against the world" attitude. In the absence of everything that nourishes the heart, the idea of attachment seems impossible and eventually, the heart stops caring in order to survive.

And so, on that June night, as I reminded myself that it had been nearly a decade since I'd been in any kind of trouble that might send me back to the hole, I got dressed and followed the officers to the infirmary to give someone else what I had craved for so long and been denied— human empathy.

The infirmary is an approximately 800-square foot ward with 20 beds arranged less than three feet apart. That night almost every bed was occupied. The air is refrigerated. The infirmary is the only air-conditioned room in the prison for prisoners. The room smells of unwashed bodies, disinfectant-mopped floors and human decay. I hear labored breathing, groans. There upon what I fear will be my future deathbed, lay an older Hispanic man who spoke no English. He was writhing in pain. He was shivering. I piled blankets on him and prayed he was warm. Because I was unable to communicate in Spanish I simply held his clammy hand while wondering about his story. Who was he? What course through life led him here? Did he have family? What were his lessons and final thoughts? I wondered if he had time to resolve his regrets and make amends for his wrongs. In the absence of words I became more sensitive to the power of presence and consciously tapped into feelings of compassion hoping the energy would resonate with the stranger as he occasionally reached to the sky and spoke in Spanish. I wanted to snatch him up in a hug close enough that my strength and vitality could hold him, at least through the night.

When morning came and another volunteer arrived for his shift, I left the room. But the man remained in my thoughts as I went through my daily routine. Later that day while training for a half marathon, it struck me as unconscionable to be so healthy and spend so little time taking care of the sick. I decided to use the strength I had to help the weak. The idea enriched my heart with a sense of purpose. Ironically, just a few hours before I had been called to sit vigil, I'd been lying in bed, heartbroken, devastated and without hope.

On May 12, 2015, Ninth Circuit District Court Judge, Thomas T. Coffin, had dismissed a civil suit seeking the possibility of release for Oregon inmates who can demonstrate rehabilitation, yet serve de facto life without parole sentences for crimes they committed as minors. This had been my best chance for a meaningful opportunity to prove myself worthy of release. I could no longer dream of planting community gardens, running the Hood to Coast relay race, raising puppies, working in the field of water conservation and volunteering to mediate conflict. The Judicial confirmation of an imprisoned death denies the greatest hope for a redemptive legacy and restoration with society.

Two weeks after the judge's ruling, an important friendship of years ended for unknown reasons. No explanation, no communication, no goodbye: just gone. Prison burdens the bonds of relationships in ways that make lasting love an impossible dream. But although a prisoner knows that most companions come and go, abandonment and loss can break even the seasoned captive's guarded heart. I laid down and wept. My light had dimmed and seemed to vanish. But one night of opening my heart to a dying stranger changed my perspective. The realization I could reasonably expect to live through the day with good health shifted my focus away from my own problems. Helping him helped me. The fears and doubts I'd had about participating in the hospice program disappeared.

I never saw the Hispanic man again, but shortly thereafter met Gus who was told by the doctors in late August of 2015 that his cancer was incurable and that he had a month to live. He agreed to enter hospice in the beginning of September.

Two days later, another hospice volunteer and I went to the infirmary to meet him for the first time. As we entered the room, Gus quickly got up out of bed and shook our hands so firmly that I was shocked a terminally ill 63-year-old man could squeeze a hand so tightly. In the first minutes of conversation I noticed that Gus's words were badly slurred; blood trickled out the corner of his mouth, and his breath was foul. The failed cancer treatment had left open sores inside his mouth, and the tumor in his throat made it difficult to swallow. Brushing his teeth was no longer an option. At first I was repulsed and automatically flinched in withdrawal. But then I realized this was a part of his struggle. I steeled my resolve and never backed away again.

Everyday I visited Gus for three hours, except on Fridays when I'd stay for six. It was painful for him to speak, but he realized that soon he would be unable to speak at all, and so he felt compelled to express his insights while talking about his life: A childhood filled with laughter; a father who was harsher on him than his younger siblings; work; vacations; outdoor adventures; how disconnected my generation is from the world around us; and how he believes so many people in prison are angry because they are actually hurting deep inside.

Although we talked about all sorts if things, Gus's favorite topic was the people in his life. "My kids are beautiful people," he often said, as he told countless stories about Ida, Sarah, Josh, Kyle, as well as his other kids and grandkids. Prisoners in hospice are allowed to have their families enter the prison for a special visit in the hospice room. Gus's three oldest were able to visit him, and he introduced me to them as the friend who wrote letters for him. Teary-eyed, his kids shook my hand while offering thanks. Now I had faces to place with the names in Gus's stories. I often forgot that because of his mental sharpness and the way he made his stories so vivid with exaggerated gestures, that he would soon be dead. Once he nearly fell from the bed while demonstrating a diving catch he'd made to keep his son Kyle from falling off a boat. He was dying but he was full of life.

As Gus would speak about the love for his kids and the things he wished he had done better, I thought about what it would have been like to have a loving father—or any father. I do not know who my father is, nor did I have any constant, positive male role models growing up. After the death of my grandmother, who had raised me with love and good values, a grandpa who beat his woman and uncles who sold weed, committed petty thief and committed assaults became my idea of how men were suppose to act. At my grandmother's funeral, I remember walking away from the lowered coffin at age twelve and hearing my uncle tell my coach how proud he was of me for dealing with it like a "little man." He meant I didn't cry or show emotion. That was what being a man meant. The years I spent in Portland, Oregon, living with my uncles at age thirteen and fourteen and then, in the streets at fifteen and sixteen where I sought to impress aspiring thugs by stealing cars and selling drugs, followed by spending most my twenties in the hole, had made me an expert in stifling my feelings. To hear Gus reflect on how he could have been a better, more loving, father made me admire the fact that he was there for his kids at all.

One of Gus's greatest sources of joy was reuniting with and reestablishing friendships with Dale, his first wife, whom he loved his entire life. Gus had been married three times. His last wife was "crazy;" his second was a "good woman but we were too different." When he spoke of Dale, the mixture of joy and pain was obvious. Pressured by her family, she'd left him, but he never told me why. There must had been significant adversity for Dale to leave and take their kids. There were periods of their lives from which he was absent, yet in the man's final days he chose to speak of the good without mention of what spilt them. After she and the kids had gone he "cried and cried" and then sought to drown the sorrow in alcohol. He admonished me sternly to never start drinking away sadness. I assured him that, even if it were available, I would not attempt to wash away woes with whiskey but rather use them as the substance of poetic stanza. Gus lifted his eyebrow and gave a half approving nod, satisfied that I swore off alcoholic solutions but not enthused about the idea of poetry. As a rugged outdoorsman, truck driver, and athlete he believed poetry "somewhat girly." However, he always wanted to hear the poems I wrote and listened intently as I read the works of Khalil Gibran, Rumi, Hafiz, Gwendolyn Brooks, Gloria Aduzula, Shakespeare and other favorite poets.

"What is a lesson that you want your son Josh to remember?" I asked, before readying myself for the painful process of his reply that I would write to share in letters to his family. Before answering, he would sit in deep contemplation with his gaze fixed somewhere far off, as if looking back across space and time into different realms before embracing the sufferance to speak:

"Always avoid"
cough cough hack
[2 minutes later]
"situations that are not good for you"
cough cough hack
[2 minutes later]
"in your thoughts and heart."

After the five minute speaking tribulation, I would read back his words as confirmation: "Always avoid situations that are not good for you in your thoughts and heart." He nodded. Much of his wisdom was laced with the distinct insight of realizing what would have been better in the first place—too late.

I was his final earthly companion, and he shared with me his most intimate thoughts and final regrets as he attempted to convey profound insights in simple words uttered with excruciating effort. Gus became the embodiment of poetry. Short verses packed with powerful reflections on love, life, heartbreak and death expressed not as fanciful prose but in short, simple phrases. Few speak as thoughtfully in life as he did in dying.

We spoke a lot about women. Where my experiences were few, his were vast. My encounters with sex as a young teenager were wrapped up in a cycle: roaming the street at night, stealing cars, partying, having sex with girls who'd trade their bodies for compliments. When I shared my stories about spending nights on the street after being kicked out of my uncle's place so he could have a woman over, and how I ran around with other delinquent kids who had nowhere else to go, he listened carefully and responded with wisdom and advice born of experience.

One day, I told him about the judge's denying me a chance of freedom and redemption. It might seem obvious to someone else that I should do all I can to achieve a better life beyond these walls, but decades of denials—lost court battles, depleted funds, inadequate resources, and emotionally exhausting legal proceedings—have taken their toll on my ability to persist against the odds. Sometimes I feel so overwhelmed that surrendering to my circumstances almost seems appealing. But Gus remained optimistic saying, "Promise you'll keep trying—one day you'll have a chance." I made the promise.

As the tumor grew up behind his eye and prevented his eyelid from closing, his eye became infected and his vision diminished, so I took it upon myself to read him the letters from his kids and Dale. One particular note from Dale was his favorite. She called him Augie (his real name was Augustine) and written on small, flowery, perfume-scented stationary were nineteen words:

"Dear Augie, I will never forget the happiness we shared and cherish our children. I will always love you."

I would often arrive to our visit to find him sleeping with Dale's love note in one hand and a family portrait on his chest. When he awoke we would write response letters, as I recorded the words he choked out to convey to his daughter the importance of pursuing her dreams, or to tell Dale that his favorite memories included trips to Disneyland with the kids in the Corvette. At the conclusion of these letters, he made a point of telling people that he still pulled himself up to pee, a declaration indicative of his sense of autonomy.

Gus was fiercely independent. At the beginning of his hospice time he'd insist on doing everything himself-cleaning the room, changing his clothes, showering, getting stuff out of drawers—and he always made me leave the room when he had to take a piss. As he weakened, he began using a hand-held urinal bottle, and the simple act of standing up to take a leak became a monumental task. First, he'd maneuver around his IV tube and grab a hold of the bed railing to pull himself up into a sitting position. Pausing to stabilize himself and catch his breath, he'd slowly reach around with one hand in search of the urine bottle while the other hand stayed firmly affixed to the railing. Once gathered, he'd slide his legs off the edge of the bed and again silently stabilize himself. Focusing on his legs, he'd begin the laborious struggle to stand up. Rarely making it up on the first attempt, he'd typically rise five or six inches before crashing down to the bed. Undeterred, he'd repeat the process until he'd completed the Herculean effort of getting, and staying, upright long enough to empty the tiny amount of fluid in his bladder.

Gus's pride compelled him to accomplish a feat that lasted no more than a minute and left him exhausted and choking, but also enlivened by the knowledge that he could do it on his own. It is that same sense of pride that compelled him to tell others, as if sharing it in his letters gave his loved ones a way of witnessing his strength.

Of course, there were times when Gus was deeply sad, but that's not how he wanted to spend his final moments. As his energy decreased, words became fewer, his pain increased, and his light grew dimmer. But his hopes remained high. Every day Gus spoke of what we'd do when he felt better: watch the Lord of the Rings trilogy in its entirety without him falling asleep; drink orange juice; listen to Bob Marley; look at his pictures again. Deteriorating daily, but now two weeks beyond the "month at max" he was given to live, Gus was so hopeful that he purchased vitamins from the prison commissary.

I watched Gus fade day after day. Now the times were more frequent that he hurt too much to speak, except for begging the nurses to end his suffering and to help him die with dignity. The State of Oregon has had a death with dignity law since 1997, but the state's Department of Correction does not recognize it. While his pain was so intense that death might have seemed a relief, his plans for when he felt better led me to believe that his spirit wanted to live. Having never witnessed such suffering, I was forced to wrestle with the idea of allowing the terminally ill to end their own lives, concluding that his death should be his final act of autonomy. But all they could do in prison hospice was increase his morphine so he was able to sleep most of the time when I wasn't there with him. Somehow, the nurses said, he would always wake up just before I'd arrive.

In late October, when his ability to speak was nearly gone, he sat gazing more intently than normal as I eagerly prepared to write his piecemeal utterance. Suddenly, he burst forth a simple statement:

"I'm innocent."

Cough, Cough.

"My kids know and I want you to know."

The choking that followed was so violent that I thought Gus might actually die right then, as he coughed up a bit of internal tissue the nurses later speculated to be a piece of esophagus. "I believe you," I said.

I never asked why he was incarcerated because it never mattered to me. Over the final months of his life as he was coming to terms with his imminent death he spoke candidly and frankly, with painful labor he spoke slowly about many of his regrets, shames, and flaws. He spoke with such honesty; I never questioned the sincerity of his deathbed reflections.

On Thursday, October 29th, Gus was sleeping when I arrived. He had begun sleeping more during our visits, so I would clean the room, empty his urine bottle, and sit bedside thinking about my own existence until he woke up. The cancer had eaten through his skin, and the flesh had begun to decay, emanating an overwhelming stench and attracting flies that I would spend hours swatting away, from both the hole in his neck and the one eye that could no longer close. However, on this day there was also a strong urine smell. I searched for spots where the urine bottle may have spilled before realizing that Gus had pissed on himself. Later that night, Gus was unresponsive to the nurses' evaluation and had begun an arrhythmic breathing pattering known as "agonal breathing" that resembles gasping and is caused by the lungs shutting down. This is usually an indication that death is very near.

A vigil was called. In the dark I sat next to the bed holding Gus's hand, while realizing that up to this point I was unknowingly hoping he would miraculously get better. Once, I had found a dying plant stuffed behind the cabinets in the prison chapel and nursed it back to life with water, loving energy, and reggae music. I was secretly hoping the same would work for Gus, so all night long I played Bob Marley's songs and poured energy into willing him through the night. Being fans of Bob Marley's music was the first commonality we had discovered early in our interactions. We both appreciated Bob's message that only love could conquer hate, set to mellow beats in socially conscious songs. It is said that a person's hearing is the last function to shut down. That night the infirmary sounded like a concert. That night I remembered plans I'd made to take my own life while in solitary confinement, desperate to escape the depression that overwhelmed me about my crime and the hopelessness of my existence. Over the past decade of healing and creating meaningful relationships I came to fall in love with life's preciousness, but once again I was confronted with thoughts of the afterlife. Before knowing Gus, I'd believed the spirit would always exist as some form of energy. But as his life force faded, I wondered more deeply about the nature of the soul. I am now further from any conclusions than ever before.

Around noon the next day the doctor came in, listened to his breathing and shined a flashlight in. "He'll be dead within minutes," he said to me in the same tone a mechanic might use when speaking about a carburetor. The muscles of my upper body tightened my chest, squeezing at my heart, and my legs felt unstable as I stood there looking at Gus. The doctor's delivery of news was something I have long accepted: prisoners are often treated dismissively, as less than human, but it enraged me that any person could speak so coldly about the final moments of another. Swallowing the lump in my throat and blinking back tears, I called out an eloquent response of "screw you" as the doctor left.

Ignoring three-hour shift rotation rules, I stayed by Gus's bed all day and into the night. An older inmate named John, who had been imprisoned 43 years earlier at the age of 19, was the senior volunteer in the hospice program and occasionally stopped by to see if I needed a break, but I didn't. There was no way I was going to leave Gus's side. So I sat staring at Gus, writing poems, drinking coffee and fighting sleep. Years of solitary confinement had taught me much about waiting, and I was determined to stay with Gus until the end.

After two days of not moving and nearly twelve hours beyond "dead in minutes," Gus suddenly flopped towards the bed's edge and fell forward. He was trying to stand up. Barely catching him and preventing a face plant onto the floor, I wondered if this was it. I then realized that Gus was pissing on both the floor and me. Back in bed, he made some half gurgling and half raspy whispering noise resembling a failed vocalization. I was ecstatic to see him alive and grabbed his hand and asked if he could hear the music. I was playing Bob Marley's "No more trouble." He squeezed my finger so feebly that I wondered if it was just my imagination, but I believe that it was Gus's last conscious act of will.

In the week that followed, Gus was in diapers. He needed to be turned to relieve the pressure on his bedsores, which had gotten so bad that the bones were visible through his rotting flesh. Cleaning him up, turning him gently, wiping ointment on his open wounds, squirting drops of water into his mouth with a medical turkey baser were humbling moments that demonstrated the true value of tenderness and attentive care. The desire to be gentle was so overwhelming that I began to understand the deep human need to ease difficulty for those we care about—and how the most basic gestures of kindness can be the most meaningful.

The medical staff was amazed that Gus was still alive. He'd had no fluids in over a week, no solid food in three months, no liquid meal replacements in almost a month, and was taking twelve breaths a minute. Nurses remarked that he was waiting for something; the doctor said it was a medical oddity. I said it was love and Bob Marley. He survived nine days beyond "dead in minutes" and each night and most days—minus three to four hours of sleep while John was there—sat with him, playing music, silently reflecting on life, and swatting away flies. At one point, a bird flew into the room through a barred but screenless window that looks out over the prison yard where the sounds of men playing softball and horseshoes drift up into the rooms of the terminally ill. The Bird perched on the windowsill. Earlier in the month, another bird (or perhaps the same one) had flown into the room and I had kept people from chasing it away because it might have been there for reasons beyond our comprehension. Perhaps it was the spirit of the unknown to which the Hispanic man had reached from the same bed. The bird and I sat as minutes ticked away. At times, Gus's breath would stop for half a minute. The bird flew off and Gus kept breathing.

On the morning of November 8, 2015, while changing the bandages on the hole in Gus's neck, a nurse discovered maggots coming out of the wound. She made the hospice volunteers leave until further notice. After returning to my cell, I sat and worried about Gus. Would he die alone, was somebody playing music, what if he tried to stand up and pee again, who was swatting away the flies? Outside of his friends and family, he was just an invisible man locked away. Yet, to me, he was an example of grace, a man whose spirit in the presence of death inspired gratitude in me daily. He faced the worst adversity with a sense of peace I had never before witnessed.

Despite my exhaustion, I passed that night without sleeping, ready to go if I were summoned back to the infirmary. As I lay in my cell, tossing and turning, surrounded by the snores of men whose dreams served as temporary release from their realities, I reflected on my two months with Gus and all he had shared with me. I had learned so many lessons: In the end it is as in the beginning, we will always need other people. Our lives will only be remembered by the lives we touched. Regrets are our greatest burden, but memories may prove the greatest treasures. Music helps the sick and strangers can become good friends quickly. Worry is a form of caring, yet holding on to negative energy invites woe. It is wise to cherish health, treat breath as a blessing, and embrace love as inspiration. I had now been both an inflictor of harm and a giver of care, and what I discovered was that the magnitude of harm, damage, or failure that I was responsible for in the past did not prevent my ability to do good in the present. Gus had helped me to become a source of love in the exact spot I was once a source of pain after so many years of isolation and apathy.

At 5:15 a.m., the first of thirty-two bells that signals the days' events would sound, loud as a fire alarm, and startled me out of my reverie. When the alarm bell for breakfast went off, and the doors finally opened, I took it upon myself to go straight to the infirmary, regardless of quarantine restrictions. I prepared to insist on being allowed to stay, no matter what.

I walked in. "Gus died yesterday." The officer told me.

"What time?" I asked.

"Around 3 in the afternoon."

That had been my regular arrival time. I turned and walked out the door and down the enclosed stairwell. I went to breakfast and sat alone. I watched my tears fall into my bowl of cornflakes and the tiny ripples they created as they splashed against the milk.

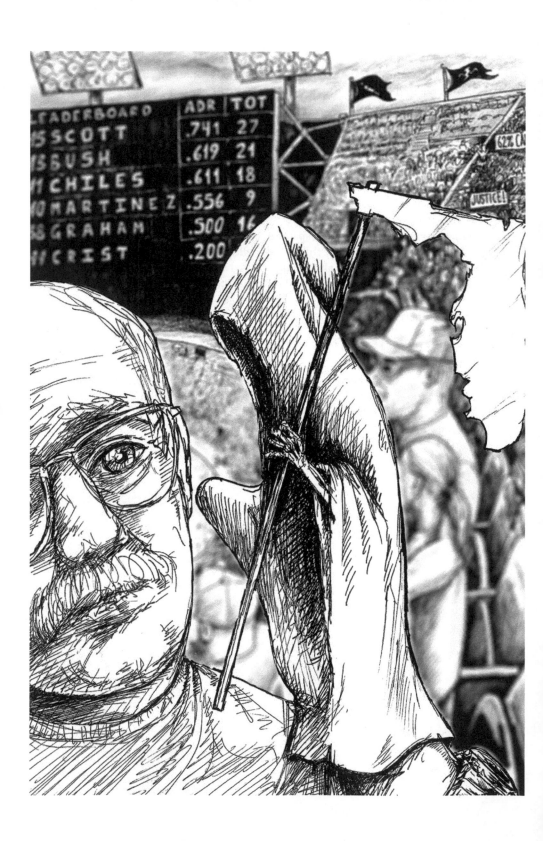

*Third Place*

# Execution Day: Involuntary Witness to Murder

## MICHAEL LAMBRIX

As if a scene straight out of The Twilight Zone, circumstances trapped me within the cold and calculated process that resulted in the murder by state sanctioned execution of Oscar Ray Bolin on January 7, 2016. In all the years I've been on Florida's death row, I've never been in such close proximity to an execution as it unfolded around me, forcing me to become part of the very process that they intended to then subject me to in precisely five weeks' time.

On November 30, 2015, Florida Governor Rick Scott signed my death warrant and I was immediately transferred from the main death row unit at Union Correctional (less than a mile away) to the "death watch" housing area on the bottom floor of Q-wing at Florida State Prison. I joined Oscar down there—his own death warrant had been signed about 5 weeks earlier and they intended to murder him on January 7. There are only three cells in the deathwatch area, and Oscar was in cell one, and I was placed in cell three, with an empty cell separating us.

Through those five weeks, each day brought him closer—his wife of almost twenty years solidly by his side, uncompromised in her commitment to stand by him and prove that he was innocent. And those familiar with the case knew that recently developed evidence did establish a persuasive issue of innocence, too.

His final rounds of appeals focused specifically on evidence supporting his innocence and the hope that the courts would do the right thing. As the New Year weekend passed, the Federal District Court summarily denied review of his innocence claim upon the finding that the lower Federal Court didn't have jurisdiction to hear his claim of innocence. But there was hope, as the District Court granted a "Certificate of Appealability" ("C.O.A.") authorizing appellate review before the Eleventh Circuit, and soon after the Eleventh Circuit issued an order establishing a "briefing schedule" in March...it seemed all but certain that Oscar would be granted a stay of execution and his claim of innocence would be fully briefed and heard by the appellate court.

Monday, January 4 passed as he anxiously awaited word that a stay of execution would be granted, but there was only silence from the court. Each day his wife spent every minute she could and it is impossible to imagine the pain she felt—she too was unquestionably a victim caught up in this cold process that unfolded around her.

I sat in my solitary cell not more than ten feet away and found myself impressed with the strength Oscar exhibited, and the concern he held for his wife and what this process inflicted on her. Society wanted to label this man a cold-blooded killer, yet if only those only too willing to throw stones could see the desperate concern he had for his wife, they could see how wrong they are.

Now I struggle to find the words—and with a reluctance to even write about what I involuntarily witnessed. But if I don't, then who will? And is it really fair that the record of what transpired would otherwise be the state's own version, leaving no perspective from those that they kill?

I must emphasize that even as much as these events impacted me due to my close proximity to the this process, it is not comparable to what they were forced to endure, and the loss those who loved Oscar Bolin suffered. My attempt to share what transpired from my own unique perspective is done in the hope that perhaps by bearing witness, others would see just how incomprehensibly inhuman this process it, and how truly cold-blooded this act of murder is...and to know it is carried out in all of our names.

And I apologize for rambling on—it is not easy for me to find the necessary words. I can only hope that I can convey the true impact of what unfolded and compel those that read this to ask themselves whether this truly is what we aspire our society to be? It's easy to justify the death penalty by claiming that it is in the interest of justice to kill those convicted of killing another—to become a killer ourselves.

But how many give a thought at all to just how much contemplation is put into this process employed to take that life? I am again reminded of what I once read, written by the philosopher Frederick Nietzsche, "Beware that, when fighting monsters, you yourself do not become a monster."

Think about that. It's easy to dismiss what I say by blindly insisting that a jury convicted Oscar Bolin of murder and that justice demands that society take his life. But really—who is actually investing more conscious thought into the act of taking a human life?

It is for this reason I'm determined to share my own unique perspective of what this process is, and how by these very actions it reduces society itself to that very level of becoming "the monster." Perhaps in my attempt to share this, others can see just how wrong this is.

On the early morning of Monday, January 4, the day began with the death watch staff advising both me and Oscar of our scheduled visits and phone calls for that day. I had already asked my family and friends not to visit that week as I didn't want my visits to interfere in any way with Oscar's visits. All I had was a phone call from my son early that morning and a legal phone call with my lawyer later that day.

Oscar had a visit with his wife and both anxiously awaited any word from the Eleventh Circuit courts hoping that a full stay of execution would come and the court would allow full and fair review of his innocence claim. But the day passed without any word from the court. By that evening Bolin was down to 72 hours—and I know from personal experience how difficult that was, as I had come within hours of execution myself when I was on death watch years earlier—only I was granted a stay.

By Tuesday morning, January 5, Oscar was down to sixty hours, and the clock continued to tick away and yet still nothing from the courts on whether they would allow his claim of innocence to be heard. Oscar spent from late morning until mid-afternoon with his wife in the non-contact visiting area. Upon his return, his demeanor was more subdued and the stress and anxiety he felt became all but tangible. And as I sat silently a few feet away in my own solitary cell, I wondered whether any of those willing to take his life gave even so much as a moment of thought into what they were inflicting upon other human beings—and again, Oscar was not the only one forced to count down those final hours anxiously hoping that phone would ring with the news that the court would allow his claim of innocence to be heard...every second of every moment, every hour that passed inflicted incomprehensible pain upon his wife and those that cared for him.

That evening passed in an uncomfortable silence as the courts would have closed their doors for the night and no news would come until at least that next morning. That psychological trauma of uncertainty weighed heavily upon them.

I doubt Oscar slept much that Tuesday night—I know I didn't. His T.V. remained on into the early morning hours. By that next morning (Wednesday) he was down to about thirty-six hours until his still scheduled execution and still no word from the court. It would be a long day. They brought the breakfast trays as they did each morning, but neither of us had any interest in eating.

Down here on deathwatch, our meals are kept under direct supervision of security staff to ensure nobody (other prisoners or staff) has any chance of tampering with the food or smuggling anything to the condemned prisoner.

This methodical countdown to the intended execution actually starts a full week before, when they remove all personal property from the condemned prisoner's cell, placing him (or her) on "Phase II." From the moment they place the condemned prisoner on Phase II (that final week) a guard is posted directly in front of the cell twenty-four hours a day, his only job to observe the condemned prisoner to ensure he (or she) doesn't attempt suicide or harm themselves—and a few have tried. Any activity is written in a forest green "Death Watch Log." Throughout this time, not even for one second are you allowed to forget that they are counting down your last days—and last hours.

Oscar again had a visit with his wife as she stood faithfully by him spending every moment she could—even if those visits were restricted to a few hours of non-contact (through glass) visits.

By early afternoon Oscar returned to his deathwatch cell—still no word from the court. The hours dragged by as Oscar talked to the guard stationed in front of his cell, simply talking about anything at all.

Warden Palmer came down, accompanied by Deputy Secretary Dixon (the second highest Department of Corrections employee). They talked to Oscar for a while mostly just to check on how he was holding up. But the preparations had begun and that final twenty-four hours was quickly approaching. After they talked to Oscar, they stepped that few feet further down to the front of my cell and spoke to me.

I must admit that I was impressed by their professionalism and their sincerity that bordered on genuine concern. Perhaps the most heard expression on death watch is an almost apologetic "we're just doing our job" and the truth is that the current staff assigned to work the death watch area and interact with the condemned prisoners counting down their final hours to do to great lengths to treat us with a sense of dignity and respect seldom even seen in the prison system.

The significance of this cannot be understated. I've been down here on death watch before years ago and came within hours of being executed myself, and there's always been a deliberate distance between the condemned and the staff—especially the higher ranking staff. But it's different this time. In the five weeks that I've been down here almost daily high ranking staff have come down to the death watch housing area and made a point of talking to us in an informal manner, abandoning that implicit wall of separation between them and us.

And now none other than the Deputy Secretary himself personally came down to talk to us—I've never heard of this before. Shortly after they left, Oscar asked the sergeant for the barber clippers. He wanted to shave his own chest and legs, rather than have them do it the next day. It had to be done, as the lethal injection process requires the attachment of heart monitors and Oscar preferred to shave it himself—as most would.

Oscar received another legal phone call later that afternoon—now down to almost twenty-four hours until his scheduled execution and still no decision by the Eleventh Circuit as to whether or not they'd allow review of his innocence claim. The lawyers would call if any news came, but it was assumed that the judges deciding his fate already called it a day and went home. No further phone call came that night. Again Oscar stayed up late, unable to sleep until sometime in the early morning hours and he was not alone, as sleep would be hard to come by.

We reached the day of execution. Typically, they change shifts at 6:00 a.m. working a full twelve-hour shift. But on days of scheduled execution, they change shifts at 4:30 a.m., as with the execution scheduled at 6:00 p.m. they cannot do a shift change then, as the entire institution will go on lockdown during that time.

With that final twenty-four hours now counting down, each minute was managed by strict "Execution Day" protocol, and the day started earlier than usual. As if an invisible cloud hung in the air, you could all but feel the weight of this day, and it was that tangible, and undoubtedly more so on Oscar. But he was holding up remarkably well, maintaining his composure even though the strain was obvious in his voice. How does one go about the day that they know they are to die? Again, I've been there myself and I know how he felt and it cannot easily be put into words.

Oscar was diabetic and as with each morning, the nurse came to check his blood sugar level and administer insulin, if necessary. Now within that final twelve hours, nothing would be left to chance. Around 7:00 a.m., they let Oscar take a shower, and then after locking down the entire institution, they took him up front for a last visit with his wife. They would be allowed a two-hour non-contact visit until 10:00 a.m., then an additional one-hour contact visit—the last visit before the scheduled execution.

Shortly after 11:00 a.m. they escorted Oscar back to the Q-Wing death-watch cell. A few minutes later "Brother Dale" Recenelli was allowed to come down and spend a few hours with Oscar as his designated spiritual advisor. Contrary to the Hollywood movies depicting the execution process, the prison chaplain is rarely, if ever, involved as each of us are allowed to have our own religious representative—and many choose "Brother Dale" as he is well-known and respected amongst the death row population.

Many years ago Brother Dale was a very successful lawyer, making more money than most can dream of. But then he experienced a life-changing event and spiritual transformation, as chronicled in his book "And I Walk on Death Row." Brother Dale and his equally devoted wife Susan gave up their wealth and privilege and devoted their lives to their faith and ministering to death row.

Even as these final hours continued to count down, I remained in that solitary cell only a few feet away and unable to escape the events as they continued to unfold around me. There are only three cells on death watch and I found it odd that they kept me down here as they proceeded with this final process—when I was on death watch in 1988, they moved me upstairs to another cell removed from the death watch area as they didn't want any other prisoners in the death watch area as these final events unfolded.

Brother Dale left about 2:00 p.m. and the death watch lieutenant, a familiar presence on death watch, then made a point of talking to Oscar and they went over the protocol—shortly before 4:00 p.m. he would shower again and then be brought around to the west side of the wing where they only had one cell immediately adjacent to the door that led to the execution chamber. I listened as this process was explained, knowing only too well that in precisely five weeks I would be given the same talk.

The warden and Asst. warden came down again and talked to Oscar. A few minutes later the Secretary (director) of the Florida Department of Corrections, Julie Jones, personally came to Oscar's cell and sat in a chair and talked to him—I've never heard of that happening before. But her tone of voice and mannerisms reflected genuine empathy towards Oscar, and he thanked her for taking that time to talk to him.

As they now closed in on that final two hours before the scheduled execution, Oscar received another phone call from his lawyer—the Eleventh Circuit Court of Appeals still had not ruled on whether they would grant a stay of execution and allow a full review of his pled innocence claim. Oscar's voice was obviously stressed. Per protocol, the nurse gave him 5 mg. Valium to calm his nerves.

Just before 4:00 p.m., Oscar spoke to me, wanting to talk about a problem he and I had years ago—a problem that I alone was responsible for and of which I have often regretted. In the five weeks we had been on deathwatch together, it was not spoken of. But now, to my amazement, even dealing with all that he was dealing with, Oscar wanted me to know that he forgave me for what I did. And for a few minutes we talked. And then the warden and his staff removed Oscar from his cell and escorted him around to the west side of the wing, to the execution chamber holding cell, where he would remain until the court cleared the way for execution, or he received a stay of execution and was brought back to this side.

A single sergeant remained on this side, and for the first time since I was brought to death watch I was along as the sergeant remained at the desk just outside the cell block area—and I didn't want to be alone. As I do often, especially when stressed, I paced in my cell anxious to hear any word on what was going on and checking my watch almost every minute, and each minute dragged by so slowly it was almost as if time itself had stopped and I couldn't begin to imagine what Oscar and his wife were going through.

At irregular intervals the sergeant would walk down to my cell to check on me and I asked whether there was any more news. The Eleventh Circuit had denied his appeal and the case quickly moved on to the U.S. Supreme Court. The designated time of scheduled execution—6:00 p.m.—came and went without any word from the Supreme Court.

Oscar would remain in that holding cell until the Supreme Court cleared the way for execution—but at least both he and his loved ones still had hope as the minutes continued to tick away.

Most don't realize just how many people are involved in this execution process and everybody remained on hold knowing whether the execution would proceed or not. Immediately adjacent to my cell was a solid steel door that led directly into a hallway stretching the entire width of the wing. Just inside this door was an area with a coffee pot and chairs, and I could hear a number of unknown people congregated only a few feet away from me on the other side of the door as they discussed the continued uncertainty.

A larger crowd of unknown participants congregated on the lower quarter-deck area between the west side of the wing where the death watch housing area was and the door that led into the east side where Oscar remained in the holding cell. I couldn't make out what they were saying and wondered, especially when I periodically heard laughter. I suppose this long wait was stressful on them, too, and a moment of levity could be forgiven. And yet I found myself wondering what they could possibly find funny as they awaited that moment of time when they would each assume their assigned task and take the life of another human being.

One hour passed, and then another, and another yet. Then at almost 10:00 p.m. it suddenly got quiet—very quiet. All the voices that continuously hummed both behind that steel door and the quarterdeck area just suddenly went silent and without anyone around to tell me; I knew that they all moved to their positions in the execution chamber.

It remained utterly silent—so quiet that I could hear the coffee pot percolating at the sergeant's desk on the other side of the gate and I held my watch as the minutes passed and I strained to hear any sound at all. But there was nothing and I knew they were now putting Oscar to death. I cannot explain it, but I just felt it—and I got on my knees and I prayed, and yet I couldn't find any words and found myself kneeling at my bunk in silence for several minutes.

Then I heard what sounded like a door on the other side of that concrete wall that separated my cell from the execution chamber. Then I once again heard muffled voices on the other side of that steel door. It was over and it went quickly...Oscar was dead. A few minutes later I heard the sound of a number of people going up the stairs leading away from the execution chamber. Their job was done and in an orderly manner they were leaving.

For obvious reasons, I didn't sleep that night. Only a few feet behind that wall of my cell, Oscar's body now lay growing cold. There are no words that can describe how I felt, but that emptiness that consumed me and left me lying in my bunk in complete silence through the night.

Somewhere in the early morning hours I fell asleep, only to awaken just after 7:00 a.m. It was a new day. The deathwatch Lieutenant was already here and I was now the only one left on deathwatch. But just that quickly, I was instructed that I had to immediately pack my property as they had to move me to cell one—the cell that Oscar only recently vacated.

I didn't want to move to that cell, but I didn't have any choice. That was the same cell I had previously occupied in late 1998 when I myself came within hours of my own execution and especially knowing that only a few hours ago Oscar was in that cell still alive and holding on to hope, I just didn't want to be moved to that cell. Every person who has been executed in the State of Florida in the past forty years was housed in that cell prior to their execution.

But it wasn't a choice and I obediently packed my property and with the officer's assistance, I was moved from cell three to cell one. And as I worked on putting all my property back where it belonged (storing it in the single steel footlocker bolted firmly to the floor), a long-awaited phone call from my close friend Jan Arriens came through.

While on deathwatch, we are allowed two personal phone calls each week, and since my warrant was signed five weeks earlier, I had anxiously awaited the opportunity to talk to Jan, but through the Christmas holiday he was visiting his family in Australia. Having only recently returned to his home in England, he arranged this phone call.

It was good to hear a friendly voice just at that time when I most especially needed a friend. But we only had a few minutes to talk and unlike those eternal moments of the night before, these minutes passed far too quickly. But just hearing the voice of a friend comforted me.

Shortly after that phone call, I then had a legal visit and was escorted to the front of the prison to meet with my lawyer's investigator. We spent hours going over legal issues and then it was back to the deathwatch cell. Not long after I returned, I learned that the governor had already signed another death warrant. This machinery of death continued to roll along. By mid-afternoon a familiar face was brought down to join me...Mark Asay (who we call "Catfish") had his death warrant signed that morning, with his execution scheduled for March 17, exactly five weeks after my own scheduled execution.

With the methodical precision of a machine, Florida has resumed executions with a vengeance, establishing a predictable pattern of signing a new death warrant even before the body of the the last executed prisoner has grown cold.

Now I remain in the infamous "cell one," next in line to be executed— and on February 11, 2016 at 6:00 p.m., the State of Florida plans to kill me. Until then, I will remain in a cell in which the last twenty-three occupants, without exception, resided until their own execution. I do not like being in this solitary cell.

# POETRY

# Grace Notes

*Matthew Mendoza*

If there is a place of grace
It is not here
Beside this seasonal stream.
The water does all the things
That water does—
Burble, trickle, rush and roar
Like the moments of our days become lives
Wearing us smooth.
We are not river stones.
There is no grace here.
This is just water.
Just like food is not love
And washing your hands
Of the heart's stains is just a myth.
Forgiveness does not flow like water.

It's fall. It's always fall now.
Leaves are not hands.
Still I read their palms.
My fingers drift along
The frame of the still leaf.
I tell the leaf,
Sometimes you are outgoing.
Sometimes you are wary.
You find it scary to reveal too much.
The trees share decades
But their leaves are short–lived.
Forgotten moments
Frozen in an orange fire.

I practice forgiveness and gratitude
And mumble a jumbled prayer
As I set the leaf sail.
I follow the glassed glide
Of its early journey.
Then, as I stumble over
Dirt, beer cans, condoms
This becomes a mirror of my own life.
The stem, like dreams,
Make an impotent rudder.
The leaf drifts past a rock.
As my leaf circles
In the eddy of a near miss
A boulder becomes a matter of perspective.

My own hurt becomes the stream.
My pain wearing smooth
The lives of people I love.
I watch the leaf
Circle, circle sink.
I go back to the place I started
And find another leaf.
If this one sinks
I'll find another.
I know that this stream is not
Forgiveness
Or goodness
Or grace
But it is only water I have.

# discovery after twenty years in prison

*Sean J. White*

Sometimes I fear
I might be
A sociopath
I have such
A propensity
For violence
Whether actual
Physical assault
The dream of it
Or bare-toothed
#
Aggression
The only thing
People seem
To understand
When wolves
Were reintroduced
to Yellowstone
Herds of ruminants
Clumped closer
Together
#
This morning
I attacked
A collection
A woman wrote
for/about
Her autistic son
My jaw ached
Fighting back tears
###
191216

# The Glitter Squirrel in Me

*Elizabeth Hawes*

You
bring out the Glitter Squirrel in me

The reading dreamer
The yearbook's class clown
The nacho-eating Twin's fan

You
bring out the Glitter Squirrel in me
the I spent my whole cheque on your Christmas present in me
the vegetarian who gets pork chops for her birthday in
me

the Captain Crunch iceberg lettuce Wonder Bread with mayo
American
cheese slices in plastic vanilla ice cream with Hershey's syrup
Hostess cupcake and 2% milk in me

the four season skin and clumpy mascara
housing laughing crescent blues in me

the negative B blood donor
Black. plastic. flecks. of white alyssum in me
the chalkboard paint on the front flower box
announcing how many soldiers died in Iraq today in me

the plaid shirted tilled fields of the Red River Valley
spring/durum/winter wheat planter
"the grass doesn't need to be mowed yet"
oil-changing, dog-loving, omelet-eating
Libertarian You, yes you
mono-browed
golden-heart cyclist of the North

You bring out the Glitter Squirrel in me
the otter & the cat cuz I tell everyone
I'm Ragstock but now Nordstroms in me

The 12 pack a day of Tab for 20 years in me.

The lighter and blower of candles
buying Sawatdee to go pad thai with tofu
at the Nicollet location with red fans and small tables.

Wearing a Crate and Barrel badge and something black in me
the I'm not going to talk about a novelist
I'm going to be it in me.

the favorite aunt street marching protester in me
the socialist/hold my ground, I wish there were
more sense of direction in me
the I'll plant thyme and lavender garden instead
of lawn, can't change a light bulb in me

the pumps clicking on cobbles & fishnets &
everyone in Women's studies hates me in me
the punks-don't-tan, Kinks-concert in me the
thinking that whoever eats veal is a douchebag because they are in me

I am the most dedicated optimism
you ever met, the optimist who stays the course
no matter what.

I am the one you warm the car seat for. I
am the one who ate all your fries.
You bring out the Glitter Squirrel in me.
peddling tricycle to CCR
alone making crazy eights in the basement
with hair like Farrah thin Levi cords
comb in back pocket
the First Ave regular
the named after a nun
the Uptown stroll
the Violent Femmes cassette Ford 250 extend
cab vs the Vespa and Roxy music
the Stella
Artois the Qtip
lover the
arthritis
the Psychic Warrior
the Thomas Merton

You bring out the Glitter Squirrel in
me tell my life with a garage full
of stage props
and set pieces.
Closets of old
auditions And
callbacks.

My family visits me every night.
stepping into my green room before the

show left, "we got your back"
left, "you got this"

I am the one who survives to love you That is why my love is like chives
a love to recycle all thoughts lost I love so I can finish the story
the way only a glitter squirrel can.

# Fragment of a Dream: A prison passage

*Gary K. Farlow*

Four layers of cement boxes
Stacked by the waters of a creek;
Each one filled with music

A stranger sits on my bunk,
Eating a box of tiny animals.
It is his room too.

Green beans and meatballs,
In steel boxes in hot water.
A pool of brown gravy!

I accept the filled plastic,
Slouching along the steel rails,
Collecting myself from the assortment.

I find myself in the Rec.,
Once again a disaster.
A cacophony of sounds.

The large orange ball,
Like a hurling meteor.
Gravity descending.

The plastic ball bounces,
Between wooden hands on the green table.
Someone is knocking!

A sharp diamond of light
In the middle of the dark glass.
Then, "The Cosby Show!"

Theo, are you crying?
There in the dark room in the box?
Theo, are we brothers?

# The Storm

*Edward Ji*

January 2nd, 2017,
5 A.M. in the shower, our power fails.
Wet and naked and dark,
We scream.

Outside,
The sky Frankensteins over our red castle,
Like it's at war with itself
Five bolts at once, playing bright notes,
Left-right, from white chapel-steeple
To black guard-tower,
Horseshoes and snipers, race-lines
Five mile long.

They herd us out,
Stairs by flashlight, scrotums dripping.
The wind swirls,
Hot and Cold together.
They pop our cage-doors with a pry bar.
They count our faces, our bunks, our feet.
They are afraid too.
Radios and keys and voices.

Now I write, by lightning-light,
Storm-flicker, no-thunder,
Only silence.

Heavy panes, pitter-patter.
Zeus-fingers climb, one two three.
Some strands red, God knows why.
He is here, in hell's veins.
Dance sky dance.

Like the clouds are killing each other:
Battleships, anvils, Jesus Christ.
Blind with awe, I cannot sleep,
Beholding worlds within worlds, afire.

Virgin thunder, rifle shot—
Split-second sculptures, scabrous red.
We all watch, silent as a church,
As brightness gives way to rain and gray.
I'm losing the muse now,
Guess I'll retire

My pencil.
I stop
When it becomes more
About the writing than the seeing.

# Five Haiku Plus Two

*Geneva J. Phillips*

1) The sheet falls tangles
    Searching hand returns empty
    He curls around her

2) Storms blow sleeting snow
    Endless panes shimmering glass
    December fences

3) Noodle bowl steaming
    White paint flakes gently
    Flutters to earth

4) Hardsilver glinting
    Clear sunglazed deep blue day
    Plane passes over

5) Accumulation
    On shelves, empty locker
    Disposable life

1a) Boxed up letters
    One picture turned just so
    Small shred, certain scrap

2a) Razorwire ruins view
    Sun setting fire cedars
    Phoenix in the ashes

# Insanity

### M. Ophelia Vaughn

Purple mountains rise in the distance,
Disrupted by coils of razor wire
Freedom only time can purchase
Brought here, branded a liar.
Medication helped me love my cage
Bottled up, three times daily rage
Fishing for a sweet relief,
It floats down like autumn leaves
My ankles and wrist hurt so fucking bad
Cuffs and Shackles too tight
Calluses turn to bloody scabs
Too many cops to fight
Regret does not burn when the doors lock
Go to war with myself til the taser shock.
Hate, Hate, Hate
I got nothing but time to contemplate
I'd do that and more
Given the chance, I'm a felony whore
Stab me, Kill me, Shoot me, feel me
My own heart beats me.

Once I resisted writing about prison. Now, I resist resisting. My best writing is about moments of magical awareness. I refused to give voice to the monotony, the bullying, and violence that make up prison life. As more of my life is swallowed by my sentence, I realized how important it is that people understand mass incarceration and America's war on minorities and the poor...

The fear of life in prison is a powerful tool.

**—Matthew Mendoza**

# DRAMA

*First Place*

# The Bucket

## JESUS ALVAREZ, VIOREL CAPRARU, JASON CHRISTNER, STERLING CUNIO, KEY DAVIS, CHRISTIAN HAWKINS, BEN PERVISH, TROY RAMSEY, AND PHIL STOCKTON

**Cast**
Captain Placard -------------- Robert Phillips
Inmate Interpreter/Jacobi ---- Viorel Capraru
Warzone --------------------- Sterling R. Cunio
Allen ----------------------- Mr. Ben Pervish
Malik ----------------------- Troy Ramsey
Max ------------------------- Christian Hawkins
Pedro ----------------------- Jesus (Mariachi) Alvarez
Depression ------------------ Robert Phillips
JJ -------------------------- Key Davis
Jeff ------------------------ Jason Christner
Piano Man ------------------- Chip
Guard Voice ----------------- Phil Stockton

**Crew**
Assistant Directors ---------- Sterling Cunio and
                               Christian Hawkins
Sound Technician ------------- Chip
Sound Design ----------------- Christian Hawkins
Scenery/Signs ---------------- Robert Phillips
Sign Assistant --------------- JK
Director --------------------- Phil Stockton

Loneliness and the feeling of being unwanted is the most terrible poverty.
- Mother Teresa

Many thanks to:
Karuna Thompson and Avrohom Perlstein for the tireless
support. Dez and Chris for the many unsung efforts.
Kelly Raths, CO Garber, T, Melissa Meychaux and all the
other actors and classmates, teachers and staff who
cheered us on and told us what was what. And to the
Monophonics, hope to see you on the inside.

This production is dedicated to those who get lost in
the darkness.

THE BUCKET

CHARACTERS
INTERPRETER ------------ V
NARRATOR/CO ------------ Phil
SIGNMAN/DARK VOICE ----- Bob
ARTMAN ---------------- JK
MAX ------------------- Chris
MALIK ----------------- Troy
ALAN ------------------ Smoke
PEDRO ----------------- Jesus
WARZONE --------------- Dez
JEFF ------------------ Jason
JJ -------------------- Key
PIANO ----------------- Chip

*While the audience is assembling and getting seated,
SIGNMAN and one other person are finishing drawing of
the lines on the paper of the back of the cells. Once
the audience is seated, the actors enter their cells.
SIGNMAN and another actor will lay down tape, and create
the silhouette of the solitary cell. The other actors
are watching them. SIGNMAN and other actor put the
bucket and mattress in the cell.*

*SIGNMAN walks onto stage holding a sign:
SIGN: OUR PERFORMANCE IS STARTING. PLEASE KEESTER YOUR
CELLPHONES. SIGNMAN turns the sign around and it reads:*

*SIGN: CELL ORIENTATION*

*(Cheesy music plays while as NARRATOR and the
INTERPRETER walk us through the orientation. INTERPRETER
wears a cardboard sign around his neck saying: INMATE
INTERPRETER)*

**NARRATOR:** Ladies and gentlemen, we'd like to welcome you
to our theatrical presentation, our show, "The Bucket"

**INTERPRETER:** What up do? My name is Bloodbath and I'll be your inmate interpreter, breakin' it down to you in layman's terms. Prison talk, feel me?

**NARRATOR:** What you see before you is a two dimensional representation, a flattened image of a typical Solitary Confinement cell.

**INTERPRETER:** Yes, what you see before you is the concrete coffin, the SMH, IMU, DSU, the CNN, the BFF. This is the hole, the box, the Bucket. Pretty much nothing changes about the place but the name.

**NARRATOR:** Marked on the floor are the typical dimensions of nine feet by six foot cell, in masking tape.

**INTERPRETER:** Nine by six cell and small as hell. Not big. I can barely do the James Brown in here, I can bang my head against four walls in four seconds. I'd show you if it had walls, there are no walls. Otherwise how would you see into the cell, know what I'm sayin'? It's theatre. Hey, ask the fuckin' director. I just work here.

**NARRATOR:** There are no windows, and the prisoner is surrounded by walls, other than the iron bars on the front of his cell.

**INTERPRETER:** Didn't I just say. that? Walls. Other than that and the bars, they are also surrounded by cocks and socks, ass gas, and rude motherfuckers that never seem *(to Jesus)* to want to shut up when you're tryin' to sleep.

**INMATE** (JESUS): Man, kiss my ass, pendejo Bloodbath.

**INTERPRETER:** OK, sweet dreams to you too. Night-night. Hijo de puta.

**NARRATOR:** On the ground in our production, but typically approximately two to three feet from the ground, is a mattress.

**INTERPRETER:** The mattress also doubles as a yoga mat, for stretching and relaxing your body. *(He does it)* Aaah. Roll it up, sit on it for your meditation and quiet moments. *(He does it)* Nice. Unroll it and use it a shield for unwanted guests. *(He does it)*.

**NARRATOR:** In the far upstage right corner you will see a bucket. For the purposes of our performances, this bucket will represent the steel toilet built into the cell.

**INTERPRETER:** Ah yes. The toilet. The toilet serves many purposes. I'm a Cleveland fan, and this is where I take the Browns to the Superbowl. Serious. *(He reaches back and we hear the sound of a flushing toilet)* This is also my ghetto-ass segregation unit cell phone. We empty the water out the bowl and talk through the pipes. My social life would be nothin' without it, you know what I'm sayin? Whenever I need someone to talk to I call on Tyrone and we talk all night. *(He yells into the toilet)* You have a collect call from inmate Bloodbath. Will you accept the charges?

**INMATE** (KEY): Man, fuck you. I'm sleeping. Hijo de puta.

**INTERPRETER:** *(He yells into the toilet)* Again? That's all you give me? You never accept my calls. We gotta talk. Damn. *(To the audience)* Oh well. Just another lonely night in the IMU, ICU, OPP, whatever.


*SIGNMAN walks across the stage with a sign*
*SIGN: WARZONE SCENE ONE - ANGER*

*(WARZONE WILLIE doing push-ups while side voice #1 is speaking)*

**INMATE** (ALAN): Truly, each breath is a blessing, and even though we may be physically held in a place we don't want to be - we can still appreciate the beauty of our existence and find meaning in our relationships, art and God. Life doesn't have to be perfect to be wonderful.

*(An irritated WARZONE jumps up and interrupts the old man)*

**WARZONE:** HEY OLD MAN, SHUT THE FUCK UP WITH THAT BULLSHIT! All he ever does is talk about how good God is, how beautiful life is, how good people help people. MAN, SHUT THE FUCK UP! You sound like some old plantation slave nigga, preaching that pie in the sky after we die bullshit. Fool, there ain't no God, just this concrete hell. Ain't nobody fallin' for that shit. Old man, I was raised in the streets. I've seen mothers abandon their own babies for dope. Human beings is worse than animals and only the strong survive. Where's your proof of a loving god and beautiful life, huh? Where's your proof? Ain't none. AIN'T NO BEAUTY IN A WARZONE! Where all we do is shoot our enemies. Policeman shoot crook. Crook shoot crook. Soldierman shoot badman. And wild-ass kids run around shooting anybody. Where's your God in all that??

**INMATE** (TROY): What about Jesus?

**WARZONE**: Jesus? That cat ain't coming back to save anybody and if he did show up, he better have a bulletproof vest, otherwise he'll get nailed again. I'll pop him myself. Hey yo, you hear this old slave fool talk about finding art in here? Ain't no art in the bucket, just a bunch of G.E.D. dummies sit around screaming about the politics of politicians who nay one give a fuck about rehabilitation. Yet you trapped clowns sit around debating who's best for the country. Man, shut the fuck up with that bullshit. Fuck this government it ain't never cared about us. Call your slave shit art if you want to but really you just wasting your days coloring paper to keep from admitting you crazy. So I say it again: shut the fuck up with that bullshit, old man, so I can get some sleep.
(*WARZONE lays down*)

*SIGNMAN walks across the stage with a sign*
*SIGN: ALAN - FRESH AIR*

(*ALAN Laying in bunk, asleep*)

**CO**: Yard. (*Pause*) YARD!

(*ALAN wakes. He sits up, looks around, puts head in hands.*)

**ALAN**: Damn!

(*ALAN Begins to brush teeth and wash his face. CO beats keys against bars*)

**ALAN**: 10 to 10. you don't have to hit those keys, we're up. The 10 to 10 rule applies to you too. In case you don't know what that means, that means no noise from 10 at night until 10 in the morning, learn the rules. CO If you want to go to yard you'll take that agitation out of your voice. ALAN Dude, I don't care about the yard. I've been in your dungeon 8 months without yard. However, the law says that you have to give me fresh air every 30 days if I want it, and I want it.

**CO**: (*Pause*) Fine. Turn around.

(*Cuffs are put on. ALAN is escorted to yard*)

**CO**: Have fun.

**ALAN**: I will.

*(Walking around the yard cell the fresh air hits him and he smiles; relaxes)*

**ALAN:** Being up so high, looking over the wall, the air up here is so much fresher. You can tell the difference from the yards that are not above the wall, man, that cell, the air in them are so stale and dry and dreary. I don't know how they can get away with not having a window in them. You have no fresh air, no view, no wonder some people go crazy. Look at me, I'm talking to myself, Must be going crazy too. I don't know how some people think that the view of homes, life, sound is cruel. I love to see and know that there is still real life out there, if this is cruel...

*(ALAN sniffs the air and smiles)*

**ALAN:** Ooo-wee, smell that? BBQ! Oh my sweet God, that smells so good. This may be cruel, but if this is punishment, then punish me.

*(ALAN listens as music starts to play)*

**ALAN:** Ooo-wee, that's a cut.

*(Prisoner starts to sing)*

**ALAN:** Hey man, Turn it up! TURN IT UP!

**CO:** Yard in. YARD IN!

**ALAN:** I just got out here.

**CO:** You had your fresh air Mr. 10 to 10.

**ALAN:** Man, fresh air hardly had time to reach over that wall.

**CO:** Fresh air's not going anywhere, neither's that wall. Back to your house, inmate.

**ALAN:** That's not my house, or my home. That's a cell. Call it what it is.

**CO:** Fine. You can turn around, cuff up, or we can come in and cuff you up. Your choice.

*(ALAN takes a deep breath, turns around and cuffs up. He returns to his cell. Back in cell he sits on bunk, looks around and places head in hands.)*

ALAN: Damn.

*SIGNMAN walks across the stage with a sign*
*SIGN: MALIK SCENE ONE - THE WALK*

*(MALIK walks around the cell as he talks, his hands shackled behind his back)*

**MALIK:** Escorted through the cell block, the smell of human despair. *(He stops)* Ooo-wee, unwashed armpits, defecation, soggy toes and spoiled booty mingle in the air. I Keep my eyes forward because the convict code. Never look into another prisoner's cell. *(He stops)* Fuck around, you might get stabbed or flashed with genitalia in anger. I don't want to see another man's genitalia or have to stab anyone so I keep my head forward. *(He stops walking and addresses the audience directly)* This here? This is called the grave, or the tomb. Because in here you're dead to the general population. *(He walks in the cell, to audience)* Looks like I'm gonna be here a few years this time.

*SIGNMAN walks across the stage with a sign*
*SIGN: MAX SCENE ONE - THE DEBUT*

*(MAX is sitting on a bucket, oblivious to everything. He hears something, he scribbles sit on a notepad)*

**CO:** Lights out!!

*(Muttering and rumbling form the other inmates "shut up, man" "Sshh" etc. MAX lies down, but as soon as he does, he gets back up again to write something on the pad.)*

**INMATE:** Come on man, show some respect.

*(Cell block quietens down)*

**MAX:** *(Quietly)* I feel undefeatable, like I could take on the world... *(He puts down the pad and sings from memory)*

**MAX:** Nights go by and I cry, all by myself-so no one can see me. Time goes by and I try to find the reason why you left me, when you were never really here. If I could stop the hands of time on that moment you were mine, would I find the words to say, to make you stay? I'd pull the stars down from the sky, when the day turns into night; Would you find your way to me, cause it's just another night that I'll be Alone, Alone - it's just another night that I'll be...

*(The cell block noise fades slowly. Max finishes the song as he lies back down)*

*SIGNMAN walks across the stage with a sign:*
*SIGN: MALIK SCENE TWO - An Awakening*

**MALIK:** One night, an inmate chose to end his life. He
woke everyone up with a loud and chilling rendition of
the lord's prayer *(INMATE recites a piece of the Lord's
Prayer is recited)* it freaked us out. Listening to the
chaos around me, nowhere to turn. These officers had
no vested interest in helping me turn my life around.
*(He sits on the bucket)* One day, I was reading, "As a
Man Thinketh" by James Allen *(He is given a book)* and
that's when it clicked. The sleep deprivation, inmates
in conflict with each other, beating on steel toilets and
hitting on the walls all night. I knew I didn't want
this to be the rest of my life. So I began to treat my
time in the graves as if I were in school. I started
getting books *(He is given 3 books by an INMATE)* from
the library and pencils(He is handed Pencils) from the
commissary and created courses for myself in subjects
like political science, African history and religion.
But my real change came when I started to keep a
journal. *(He is handed a journal and stands with the
journal and pen)*

I began writing any time I got angry at the other
inmates and officers--What I wanted to do to them and
why. I wanted to kill some of them and others I just
wanted to really hurt bad. To me they were worthless
pieces of shit who deserved a swift and painful death or
to be beat down.

*(Movement among the INMATES, they encourage him, and he
stabs the book with the pen and throws it on the ground)*

When I went back a few days later I went back to read
what I had written. It disturbed me. All of them had
been inconsiderate no doubt, but was it a personal
attack? Even if it was, did they really deserve to be
harmed or killed? It's hard to express how much this
process of examination began to change me. For the first
time I could remember, I began to recognize my true
self. Inside me burned that same rage - rage that had
nearly cost an officer his life and me the rest of
my life in prison. Rage that had consumed me to take
a man's life while I was on the streets years ago.
Fighting for my dignity and respect. Plenty of days, I
felt like the grave would consume my spirit *(he gets the
pen and paper)*.
I clung to my sanity and wrote my thoughts. I began to
realize I had emotions I had never addressed. I wrote
about my mother. I wrote about.. I wrote the thoughts. I
wrote them all. I wrote my way out of prison.

*SIGNMAN walks across the stage with a sign:*
*SIGN: HALF-WAY POINT (APPROXIMATELY). QUESTIONS SO FAR?*
*If anyone has any questions, SIGNMAN will spend a*
*couple minutes answering them. If he can not answer the*
*question, he can turn to one of the actors to help him.*
*He flips the sign to show the next scene.*

*SIGNMAN walks across the stage with a sign*
*SIGN: PEDRO - Hope and faith*

**PEDRO:** *(Working Out)* 198, 199, 200. Come on. One more.
Come on. COME ON! *(Starts to pace back and forth)* I
can't do it. Man, I'm feeling so sad, so dark. I'm
freaking losing my mind. What's wrong with me? I'm tired
of this shit. *(He gets on his bunk and works on his*
*dream catcher)*

**CO:** Hernandez, roll up. Today's the day, you're done
here.

**PEDRO:** What? Today? No, I can't.

**CO:** You can't? Why not?

**PEDRO:** It's just...too early. I have a schedule to
maintain.

**CO:** What the hell schedule are you talking about
Hernandez? You crazy? Fine by me.

*(CO leaves)*

**PEDRO:** I'm not ready. I'm not, I can't.. *(He begins to*
*cry)* Man I'm not ready, I'm not fucking ready. It's just
too much, I can't even deal with being in: here. What's
gonna happen to me out there? Maybe I am crazy. *(He sits*
*on his bucket and puts his head in his hands. DARK VOICE*
*over the speakers and a dark presence walks on stage,*
*wearing a mask.)*

**DARK VOICE:** I'm a dark cloud. I am not prejudiced, I
take anyone. I am apathetic. I feel nothing, I care
about no one. I will not give up. I may leave but I'll
be back. I control you, I tell you what to feel. I
take your concentration, I own your energy. I own your
happiness. I am everything. I am forever.

**PEDRO:** *(Rocking back and forth)* I'm not ready, I'm not
ready.

**INMATE 1** (JASON): Hey Pedro. You had a chance to get out
and you didn't? You stupid or something?

**PEDRO:** I don't care. Leave me the fuck alone.

**INMATE 2** (V): Man, you must be stupid, or scared.

**PEDRO:** I'm not scared, kiss my brown ass.

**INMATE 3** (CHRIS): Hey Pedro, if you're scared talk to God.

**INMATE 4** (STERLING): Hug your bible, see if that'll save you!

**INMATE 5** (SMOKE): Yeah, you know, The bible saves everything.

(Inmates laugh loudly, Pedro takes the bible and punches it)

**PEDRO:** I'm not scared. I'm just not ready.

**[NARRATOR:]**
So PEDRO was saved while being in solitary confinement. Yes, he did. One night an INMATE asked PEDRO "if you were to die tonight, do you think you'd go to heaven? PEDRO said "I don't know." The INMATE then asked "Would you like to find out?" PEDRO said yes. So they started praying and repenting. Asking Christ for forgiveness. The INMATE looks at PEDRO and asks "Pedro, do you believe that Jesus died for your sins on the cross?" PEDRO said "yes" and the inmate asked one last question, "Pedro, if you were to die right here, right now, do you believe you'd go to heaven?" With a smile from ear to ear, he said "absolutely." So all he needed to do was repent, believe, receive.

(PEDRO takes his bible and stands in the center of his cell. Music begins and he steps out and begins to talk to the Audience about his revelation and Cell conversion)

**JJ:** Pedro. What you doin' man? It's too quiet. What's goin' on man?

**PEDRO:** Reading. Reading my bible.

**JJ:** What could that book possibly do for you?

**PEDRO:** Well, I don't feel depressed no more. I feel... faith and inspiration.

**JJ:** Oh yeah? How you feel that? How do you know?

**PEDRO:** It's like this. One day I saw these little ants

walking in formation, carrying a heavy load. I dropped some hot water on them by accident. It splashed down on them. Some died right away.

Others panicked, running around, not knowing what to do. But this one little ant had faith. It kept walking forward with its heavy load. Ooh, aah! ooh! The ant walked on, burning it's little feet.

I got down on his level and told him "go little ant, go! You can do it, little ant, go!" I wanted to help it by picking it up and taking it to its hole. But I knew if I did I would just crush it. So I picked up a stick, and I put it over the water and into the hole. The ant hopped onto the stick and walked straight into the hole. So, that's the story, that's how God looks down on us, you see like ants. And with faith, he can help place his stick to where we need to go. So the question is, what type of ant you want to be? You want to be the ant that dies right there, you want to be the one who loses his way, or you want to be the one with faith, who makes it?

**INMATE 2:** Can I get an Amen?

**INMATES:** Amen!

**INMATE 4:** Can I get a Hallelujah!

**INMATES:** Hallelujah!

**INMATE 1:** Haha, you're just another bible fool.

**PEDRO:** I'm a fool? You're a fool. This little ant's no fool. This little ant is walking on, and walking out. Yo. CO? I'm ready. YO CO. I'M READY.

*(PEDRO stands in his cell ready to leave)*


*SIGNMAN walks across the stage with a sign:*
*SIGN: WARZONE SCENE 2 - SORROW, 27 YEARS*

**WARZONE:** 27 years ago today, I came to prison a young thug. Angry at the world, hostile to everybody. Man, I've spent the last nine years in the bucket and the ghost of innocents murdered, they haunt me. I'm tired of it man. Tired of the regret, the wasted potential. I'm tired of sleeping alone at night, no hugs, no kissing, no cuddling. Im tired of being hungry, wishing for hot food not served through a hole in the door like some kind of feed trough. I'm tired of all the screaming and waking up everyday surrounded by hostility and misery.

I'm tired of the hatred. Its makes me weary. I'm tired
of being a prisoner. Tired of not seeing the sun. My
soul misses the moon. My humanity is stained and my
existence is spent in a tomb. I am already everywhere
I'll ever be.
It's over.

(*WARZONE hangs his head.*)

**INMATE** (CHRIS): Stay strong Warzone. Don't do it man!

**WARZONE**: Hey homie, aint' no need in trying to talk me
out of it. If I'm destined for hell I might as well
arrive on my own terms. Skip the cancers, the organ
failures, and cheat the state out of a few decades.
I just hope that some part of death is quiet and
dark--Some silence and escape these lights. Maybe in the
afterlife I find forgiveness. If I can explain with a
greater clarity that it was pain that caused me to hurt
so many.

You want my stuff or what?


*SIGNMAN walks across the stage with a sign*
*SIGN: JJ - US*

(*JJ sits on the bucket. He's looking at a real picture
of Drew Barrymore. He hums a few bars from "Falling
Apart" An imaginary phone rings, he mimes picking up the
phone*)

**JJ**: What's up girl? I've been waiting for your call.
Huh. How was your day? Busy. How's the TV show? That's
cool. Uh-huh. Been busy here too. Yeah, you know,
(*he looks around*) just bein'...busy. (*He laughs*) Uh-
huh. Yeah. Oh yeah. You know that's right. Remember
how you said I should share my feelings, get creative?
Yeah, well I got something for you. (*JJ begins singing
"Falling Apart" - The Monophonics*) Why can't it just be
easy The struggle, the struggle has gone on too long.
And what's the use in dreaming Cause everyday, everyday
I'm all alone Somebody please, will you help me Cause
I'm falling apart, I'm falling apart...

You like that? Sometimes I like to think they wrote that
for you. No, them, not me. I would've wrote it if I
could, you know I would. What? Say what? You know those
guys? Get out, you know them? Man, that's crazy. I guess
all you famous people hang together down in Los Angeles,
Huh. Yeah. Oh, I know. (*JJ Doesn't pick up the phone
again. From this point on JJ acts as if Drew Barrymore*

*was in the cell with him)* So... He's a friend, huh. That
singer cat. What kind of friend? A good friend? What do
I mean? I mean what kind of friend. I just want to know,
that's all. Oh. OK. Casual. Casual as in friend casual,
or as in let's go in the back room, you know, the one
with the king size bed and the red silk sheets, and
get casual. And then he can just touch you down there
casually and - God damn it, girl. You fuckin' that guy?
Huh? IS THAT IT? THAT'S WHY YOU AIN'T BEEN CALLING ME?
Damn!

Ok. Ok, baby. Sorry. Yeah, baby. I know,I know, I'm
workin' on it. I'm tryin'. It ain't easy. You know that.
You know that.I don't take the pills, I told you that
before. I take the pills and then you never call me or
come visit. I miss you. Drew, baby, I see you on the TV,
in those magazines, those... snapshots. I collect them
all, you know I do. Cut them out every day that I can.
This one right here's my favorite. *(Points to a space
on the wall)* You on the bike. Goin' some place. Maybe
to come see me. And then this one, and this one. *(He
reaches around, shows and touches some of her pictures
on the wall)* But the end of the day, they're all just
pictures. Nothin' but. That's all they are, baby. That's
right. It ain't you. Yeah. We know that. They don't.
They don't. But we do. But, you know, also, it ain't.
all about you, I mean... What about us? OK, yeah. But.
Listen to me. Just once. Just once, I'd like you to.
Please. I'm asking you. I'm begging you. What about us?


*SIGNMAN walks across the stage with a sign*
*SIGN: JACOBI - FRIENDS? WHAT FRIENDS?*

**INMATE 1** (JEFF): Yo, new guy, what's your name?

**INMATE 2** (SMOKE): Who you roll with, dude?

**INMATE 3** (PEDRO): Who're your friends?

**INMATE 2** (SMOKE): Hey man, you hear me?

**JACOBI:** Who do I roll with? Who are my friends? Huh.
Shit. You see this cell? This is what I got, right here.
*(He laughs)* This is my friend for now. My Cell. With
myself, Man, what the fuck is this, it's way too soon
for this shit. Are you for real? How about this shit,
is this for real? *(He looks at the audience)* Are you for
real? Let's see here.

*(He steps out of his cell and addresses members of the
audience)* Are you my friend? What about you? You my

friend? Man, I got no friends. This cell, the reason I'm here is because of my friends. This is the reflection of my reality right here. This cell is a better friend to me then the people who put me here. Look at this fuckin' place. Dirty little joke. Shit.

I had a friend one time. My so called friend dropped kites on me, got me hemmed up so his punk ass could steal my job.

Motherfucker.

Got a nice little place in the woodshop. All my own. I make nice furniture, man. Chairs and crap. Real pretty. Fancy as shit. Serious. Some dude told me the office ladies use them. Haha. That shit keeps me warm at night. *(He laughs)* Yeah. Now I'm sitting under investigation for some bullshit my fuckin' "friend" faked to snake my place… *(Pause)* Truth is, he may get it. *(Pause)*

So. Do I have friends? Hell yeah, but the friends you get is determined by the friendship you give. Hear me? Friendship requires sacrifice, time, energy. Things I been burned on. And I burn bright.

Hear me?

Trust. Shit.

Truth is, many of us are uncomfortable up close. We grew up in homes where intimacy was rare. Nowhere in sight. Communication was a form of control, and rules more important than relationships. As a result we're "relationally impaired". Friends don't come easy. So let me ask you. Straight up. Are you my friend?

*(He steps back in his cell)*

**INMATE 2** (SMOKE): Damn man. I asked a simple question. *(He laughs)*

**INMATE 3** (PEDRO): Hey yo, ese, you need to chill. Therapy hours are over. *(Sarcastically)* Besides, we just want to be your friend. *(He laughs)*

**JACOBI**: Yeah. Friends got me in here and they sure as shit ain't gonna get me out. I didn't come here with no friend and I'm sure as shit not going to leave with one.

**INMATE 2** (SMOKE): OK man, whatever. Tomorrow will be a new day. Cause I know you ain't goin' nowhere. *(He laughs)*

**INMATE 3** (PEDRO): For real. Hey new guy!

JACOBI: Yeah.

**INMATE 3** (PEDRO): Better get yourself a new speech ready. Tomorrow's question is: What is your name! *(INMATES laugh)*

*SIGNMAN walks across the stage with a sign*
*SIGN: MAX SCENE 2 - THE ENCORE*

**CO**: Chow! *(Excitedly, MAX starts writing lyrics, moving from place to place to illustrate time)*

**INMATE** (TROY): Hey, was that you singing last night? *(MAX keeps writing, singing softly)*

**INMATE** (TROY): Hey American Idol! You talk? Or do you just sing?

**INMATE 2** (DEZ): You got a song about a bitch?

**INMATE 3** (ALAN): He is a bitch

**INMATE 4** (V): Let's hear something about a female

**INMATE 3** (ALAN): He wants to sing to his boyfriend

**INMATE 2** (DEZ): Yeah, let's hear something about some girl, man.

*(MAX puts his notebook down, makes a beat on the wall and sings)*

**MAX**:
All eyes on her when she steps on the scene She got them high heels on and walks like a beauty queen; Dark hair and green eyes that take me by surprise, Every time I see her: look ma I think I caught a keeper; Five foot six and forty inch hips, silhouette is just ridiculous; just gonna kiss them thick lips, I can't resist, I must confess: I never seen anything in jeans that look a thing like she do; Hypnotized by the way she move She got that, ooh girl she got that-She got that ooh girl *(repeat)(Some cheering and clapping from the guys)*

**INMATE 3** (ALAN): Hey man, I'm five foot six.

**INMATE 2** (DEZ): I've got forty inch hips

**INMATE** (TROY): Hey American Idol, what's your name?

**MAX:** Max.

**INMATE** (TROY): That was dope, for real. You out soon?

**MAX:** (Softly) No.

**INMATE 2** (DEZ): How much time you got?

**MAX:** I got letters, I ain't got numbers

**INMATE 3** (ALAN): The fuck that mean? When you get out?

**MAX:** I'm not.

**INMATE 4:** You never gettin' out and you're singing about females? (Laughs)

**INMATE 2** (DEZ): I tell you what, I'll get out next year, I'm gonna fuck that bitch.

*(Cell block laughs, MAX goes back to writing)*

**CO:** Lights Out!

*(MAX starts singing as he's writing. Gradually the noise gets softer and music begins to get louder. We see MAX step out of his cell, stepping out towards the front of his cell. He sings a song. As the music ends he steps back into his cell and it's quiet for a moment)*

**INMATE** (JASON): Fag! *(Laughter in the cell block. MAX looks at the lyrics in the notepad, rips them out and crumples the paper)*


*SIGNMAN walks across the stage with a sign*
*SIGN: JEFF SCENE ONE - KILL YOURSELF*

*(JEFF is sitting in his cell with a paper crane. He talks to the audience)*

**JEFF:** I was 7 years old the first time my parents took me to the doctors for "it". They didn't know what "it" was, but the school nurse said I had to go. My parents didn't think it was worth the trip, they were too busy. They were always busy. My dad, he was busy looking for work. My Mom, she was busy with her soap. And today, of all the days I could have picked to have a fit, was the day that.... On General Hospital. My mom looked at me like I was a bad commercial. *(In his mother's voice)* "For Goodness sakes. Why do I have to suffer just because you're too afraid to have your picture taken?

Your father paid a lot of money for the pictures. You
asked for them". I didn't ask. "That money is coming out
of your allowance" she said. I didn't get allowance.

I said I was sorry. I said the camera hurt. It was too
bright. Like the fluorescents always on. Relentless.

*(He walks to the back of his cell, and we transition
into the cell with him. Noises begin slowly from the
INMATES. Coughs, etc.)*

*(JEFF has one of his tics)* I can see the cop in the
control station. He just came back from a smoke break.
I can tell because of the smell. The smell. The cops
like to blow their smoke in my air vent. They must
smoke on the roof, that's where the air vent goes. No
one else can even smell it, so it must just be my vent.
My vent! They do that shit on purpose. I know they do.
*(He tics)* I smell everything that happens here, hear it
too. Yes I do. The doctor said it was called autism.
One said it was called ass-burgers with characteristic
hypersensitivity. Ass-burgers, sounds like something
on a menu. Can I please have the Ass-burgers well done
with a side of shit sauce. Yum. I can smell it now. *(He
giggles and tics. He coughs.)* Cigarette smell is making
me nauseous. I can't stand it anymore. *(He tics. Pause)*

I'm smarter than they think. I know how to fight back
against the smell. I figured it out. The first time I
almost puked, but I got used to it. I have my defense,
my countermeasures, I hardly smell them anymore. Now
they have to smell my shit. It's their own damn fault.
If they fed us better food it wouldn't. smell so bad
coming out. Smells like assburgers. *(He giggles)* Don't
go thinking I'm crazy, I'm not. There's technique
involved, oh yes there's technique. You gotta put it
in the cracks. Nice and precise. Like the tiles in the
bathroom floor. Around the door, down here, and here.
Just like that. That's where you put it. And not all at
once, either. You gotta do it in layers, so they dry.
quicker. Nice and light. They gotta dry in between, or
they smear and that would be gross. And you can't skip
places either. You skip a place, their smell can get in.
And keep your lines straight, that's important, I can't
overemphasize that enough! *(He tics)* Keep them straight
and keep them proud.

*(Noises continue. Escalating slowly. A toilet flushes
loudly)*

**JEFF:** I can smell the sound, it's louder than smoke,
brighter than the lights.

**INMATE 2** (TROY): Put some water on it. (Toilets keep flushing with other sounds introduced.)

**INMATE 3** (SMOKE): It ain't me.

**INMATE 2** (TROY): I just heard you flush

**INMATE 3** (SMOKE): *(to JEFF)* Man, shut the fuck up. *(To INMATE 2)* It's my neighbor.

**INMATE 2** (TROY): You best not be playin' with your shit again, you fucking nut!

**INMATE 3** (SMOKE): You better not be!

**INMATE 2** (TROY): Damn right, don't do it. Sick and tired of that shit, and I mean your shit. *(Pause)* Just fuckin' take care of business.

**INMATE 3** (SMOKE): Yeah man, kill yourself.

**INMATES**: Yeah, man Kill yourself. You piece of shit. Kill yourself, *(etc)*

**JEFF**: What? No, stop it.

*(Chorus begins, repeating "kill yourself". other sound elements are introduced. Lights begin to shake.)*

**JEFF**: Stop it, stop it, stop it, stop it...

*(Chorus grows with intensity and tears down the paper walls behind their cells. They take the lights and point them at JEFF, who is crouching on the floor. Sound reaches a crescendo, and JEFF covers his paper crane)*

*SIGNMAN walks across the stage with a sign*
*SIGN: WARZONE SCENE 3 - PEACE, 43 IN*

*(A wheelchair is brought forward. WARZONE sits in it.)*

*(WARZONE wheels into the cell in a wheelchair)*

**WARZONE**: Good Morning all.

**INMATES**: Good morning, Warzone, what's up, etc.

**WARZONE**: How's everybody?

**INMATES**: All right, blessed, etc...

**INMATE** (SMOKE): How are them creaky bones today, Mr. Poet? You finished that poem yet?

**WARZONE**: As a matter of fact I did. Couldn't sleep last night...

**INMATE** (SMOKE): Man you never sleep any night.

**WARZONE**: I keep busy. Plenty to do. A busy mind lets the soul breathe.

**INMATE** (V): Whattaya got? Read it old man.

**WARZONE**: Well, I wrote this early morning. Let's see here, goes something like this:

In these concrete tombs
that most call cells
resistance becomes survival.
Art and creativity
Enable some to transcend negativity
Sleepless nights
The perfect time to write
Cold, hungry and alone
I draw pictures of warm places
With abundant food for many companions
Barren environment void of stimuli
One makes a garden of his mind
Planting seeds and fertilizing self-actualization
We sing songs of resistance
Heard by none because we are the voiceless
Transforming struggle to the substance of stanza
Cell block scholars
Handcuffed residency
Master degrees of captivity
Unaccredited doctorates of deprivation
With colored ink from Sunday comics and coffee-stained toothbrushes
We paint bright murals inside dark tombs
Monk like meditation reveals
Inner alchemy necessary to transform tombs to monasteries. Paranormal paradox
Instead of being spiritual crushed
We evolve in a box
Thrown in the hole and told we'll never see the sun again-
We are those who blow kisses at the moon.
Indomitable wills create artistry out of sufferance,
Even with handcuffs on wrist
We can build peace from inside the belly of the beast
And throw peace signs at the prison industrial complex.
Resistance is survival
and love our salvation.

**INMATE** (AUDIENCE): HEY OLD MAN SHUT THE FUCK UP WITH
THAT BULLSHIT!


*SIGNMAN walks across the stage with a sign:*
*SIGN: JEFF SCENE TWO - THE SILENCE*

*(JEFF walks on stage with his paper crane. He walks
around studies the cell for a moment, puts the crane
at the front of the cell and then steps in, sits on the
bucket and looks at the floor for some seconds. He slowly
raises his head and puts his hands in a piano playing
position. CHIP begins playing the piano and the INMATE
plays the exact same song in the air. As he plays, after
a few moments, The tape is removed from the floor by
the ensemble. The bucket is turned around, the tape is
thrown in and everything is removed.)*


*SIGNMAN walks across with a sign:*
*SIGN: THE END, CLAP WHENEVER.*

*There will be a talkback after the show. Actors will
take seats and the audience can ask questions which the
actors will answer.*

*Second Place*

# Freedom Feather
## MATTHEW MENDOZA

**CAST**
Major
C.O. with Billy Club
C.O. Lorraine
C.O. Durst
Miss Lanie
Inmate Lincoln
Inmate Wald
Inmate Rodriguez
Erica

**TIME**
Present day

**PROPS**
Nine plastic chairs
A bunch of red feathers
One billy club
Audubon's "Book of Birds"

*(Nine cheap plastic chairs line the stage. A parade of C.O.'s, support staff and inmates file in and take a seat. An empty chair separates the shackled inmates from the C.O.'s. A C.O. with a billy club stands behind the three inmates. A tall C.O. with a major's star looks down the row of chairs then rises and steps to the center of the stage.)*

**CAPTAIN**
I don't think anybody believes that an inmate turned into a bird and flew away. What we do know is that inmate Carlos Prospero Sanchez was last rostered at the eight-thirty count. That's A.M. The inmate can be seen clearly on the tape at that time. He seemed to be meditating. He was seen sitting on his bunk. The inmate remained on his bunk like that for an hour. At that point, there seemed to be a flash or a whiteout

that lasted thirty-seven seconds. The inmate may have found a way to tamper with the camera or tamper with his radio or other appliances in a way that caused the flash. We are still investigating that. We do know that the inmate was not present at the twelve o'clock count. After several recounts, we sent all the inmates on the farm back to their assigned housing and did a thorough search. The unit remains locked down. Local police, county sheriffs, and the Texas Rangers are actively searching for inmate Sanchez. We have two teams of tracking dogs. Several local citizens with access to small aircrafts are also aiding in the search. We currently have no leads, but we believe that inmate Sanchez will be apprehended soon.
*(The major scans the audience and returns to his seat on the end of the row. The C.O. with the billy club prods an inmate with his nightstick. The inmate jerks away, glares at the C.O. then shuffles to the center stage.)*

### INMATE LINCOLN

*(Mimics.)*
I don't think anybody actually believes that an inmate turned into a bird.
*(Street Voice.)*
I'm telling you, that man turned into a bird and flew away. He said he was gonna do it and he did it. Why you think they called him the Bird Man? You would think his people just made that up. Why you think he had that feather? I don't know how he did it. A lot of folks do that Native American thing for flavor but it was different for Bird Man. When he found that feather on the yard, he said it was from a red-taped hawk. He said that it was a sign. He said that the feather had power. To me, it just looked like a plain feather. It didn't even look red. But he believed it. He carried that feather everywhere. To the chow hall, to education, to the rec yard. He held it out to his side like sticking your hand out the bus window. You say what you want to - that's what you gonna do anyway. I'm telling you, that man found a way to make like a bird and fly away. Just like you say. He see'd it. He belee'd it. That man achieved it.
*(Inmate Lincoln shuffles back to his seat. The C.O. with the billy club prods the next inmate. Inmate Wald shuffles to center stage.)*

### INMATE WALD

I don't even know why I'm here. Yeah. Yeah. I know Bird Man was my cellie. So what? You know how many cellies I've had? Yeah. I don't either. But it was a lot. A whole lot. I don't keep track of that shit. That's your job. I do MY time. I don't do nobody else's. You know how long I've been locked up? Nineteen years. That's a

whole 'nother life. My old lady moved on. Stayed with me
for eleven years. My little bro went blind cookin' that
meth. All I do is listen to the radio. Read some books.
That Game of Thrones is what's up. I never talked to
Bird Man. I didn't reach out to him or connect with him.
Sometimes, he'd buy me a soda or an ice cream. Yeah. I
know that's not allowed. So what? Bet you won't kick me
out of prison for it. I hope he did turn into a bird on
your ass. I hope he makes your life hard. Hard as ours.
*(Inmate Wald shuffles back to the chairs The C.O. with
the billy club grabs the collar of Inmate Wald's shirt
and drags him offstage.  Inmate Rodriguez looks around,
shrugs and shuffles to the center of the stage.)*

### INMATE RODRÍGUEZ

Hey. Que tal? OK. So, one time, he told me, Someday I'm
gonna fly away. He said, "I'm gonna soar so high I'll
look around and see nada but los cielos. No razor wire.
Nada pero clouds and sky."  I asked him, Pajaro, "you
gonna take me with you?" He said, "find you a feather,
Pepe. Find you a feather." I said, "Hell no. I'm afraid
of heights."
*(Looks around.)*
I'm not afraid of them. I just don't like being
somewhere that's not on the ground or whatever. Plus, I
only got seven years. I can do seven years standing on
my head. I'll leave the feathers to those vatos who need
them.
*(Inmate Rodriguez shuffles back and sits down in his
plastic chair. The Major returns to center stage.)*

### MAJOR

Again. No one believes that inmate Sanchez turned into a
bird.
*(The Major returns to his seat. A broad in casual,
mismatched clothes and oversized glasses steps forward.
She carries a copy of Audubon's book of birds. When she
gets center stage, she opens the book and holds it up.)*

### MISS LANIE

This is a picture of a red-tailed hawk. It is
interesting to note that Inmate Sanchez—Pajaro, which
means bird in Spanish—that inmate Sanchez and the red-
tailed hawk in this picture do look similar. This
particular book is not available to be checked out,
but the inmates are allowed to read it during assigned
library time. Inmate Sanchez would spend his entire
forty-five minutes sketching or writing poems about the
red-tailed hawk.I encouraged this. I even kept one of
his poems.Yes,I know that this is not allowed, but I
found it and I kept it.I have it here.
*(Miss Lanie sets the book on the floor and pulls a piece
of paper from her pocket and unfolds it.)*

It's a haiku, really. Not a poem.
(*Reads.*)
"Each day my soul shrinks. Wind doesn't taste the same
through razor wire."
(*Miss Lanie folds up the poem and returns it to her
pocket.*)
A library is an amazing place. Entire universes all in
one little, bitty room. I encourage all the inmates
who use the library to dream big — to let their souls
breathe. I don't know if inmate Sanchez turned into a
bird or not. It is interesting to imagine, isn't it,
spending your life soaring where the air tastes the way
it should.
(*Miss Lanie picks up her book and returns to her seat.
The major holds out his hand and Miss Lanie gives him
the poem. A C.O. in a razor-sharp uniform, slick hair
beneath her cowboy hat and polished boots, marches
toward center stage.*)

### C.O. LORRAINE

Lorraine. C.O. Five. North Tower. I know what you're all
thinking. Woman, right? She's weak. She let him waltz
right on by. You would think that a woman doesn't belong
in the tower. That I don't belong up there. Well, I do.
I can outscore everyone of you on the range and I can
outshoot everyone of you beer-bellies out here and I'm
not going to miss out on a chance to prove it. It took
me five years to make it into that tower. I earned it.
If some looney-tunes inmate is dumb enough to run past
my post, he's gonna get shot. I promise you. I promise
you. If inmate Sanchez came my way, he'd have a hole in
him - not a little lady-like hole either. A regulation-
sized hole. A permanent reminder of his time here and a
lifelong limp to go with it. There is nothing weak about
this woman and I'd appreciate it if you'd remember that.
(*Steps back. Steps forward.*)
I didn't see any unauthorized birds either.
(*C.O. Lorraine returns to her seat. C.O. Durst steps
forward.*)

### DURST

Lorraine is a hell of a shot. Me? I couldn't hit water
if I fell out of a boat. I don't believe that this
inmate turned into a red-tailed hawk or any other type
of bird. Listen — truth is, I can't imagine anything
worse than being locked up. I can't imagine being locked
up myself. To look around and see nothing but concrete
and steel and razor wire. I'm not saying nobody belongs
here, but decades? Decades. Then when you release 'em
they're socially retarded and you expect 'em to be
citizens. That's funny justice. Hell, you can't release
a bear into the wild after he's been locked in a cage
for some years. A bear. That wire does something to a

man.

*(Looks back at Lorraine.)*

...and a woman. I'd go crazy myself. Sometimes I do anyway and I only work four days a week. That's long enough. Hell, most weeks it's too long. And he had a what? A twenty-five? Twenty-five years of this place. The same food every week. The same routine every day from your first day to your last day twenty-five years later. Hell, even if you teach them a trade in here, they can't do nothing with it until they make parole five, ten years down the line. Book learning is just a fantasy if you can't do nothing with it. I'd try to turn my ass into a bird, too. Not a hawk though. I like those scissor-tail flycatchers. Now that's a bird.

*(C.O. Durst returns to his seat. A woman – the victim – steps out of the audience and walks up on stage.)*

### ERICA

They told me he escaped. Warned me. Warned me? In one phone call you took everything that I built away from me. Now, you say that he turned into a bird. What am I supposed to do with that? Am I supposed to be afraid of birds now, too? Then what? Trees? I'll stay away from trees. Then grass. Will grass be next. I hate him for what he did. He deserves prison. He hurt me. He made me think that what we did was normal. But I am tired of being the victim. I'm better than that. I'm bigger than that. No one will let me be anything else. You make me the victim. I want to forgive him and move on — to accept his apology if he has one. If not, screw him. But I need to move on and no one will let me. I hope he did turn into a bird and he poops on this whole, stinky system. I'm tired of hating. I'm tired of hurting. I'm done being the victim. Justice didn't make anything better and no one will let me forgive.

*(Suddenly, shiny, red feathers drift down from the ceiling. They shimmer and twist in the light. Everyone on stage watches them drift down. Erica returns to her seat. Before she leaves the stage, inmate Lincoln and inmate Rodriguez each scoop up a feather and move toward Erica. Erica freezes in terror. The inmates stop and offer Erica a feather. After a moment, Erica steps towards the inmates and takes a feather from each of them. She squeezes their hands and leaves the stage. The C.O. with the billy club herds the inmates back to their seats. The Major stands and walks to the center of the stage.)*

### MAJOR

I think that it is important to remind everyone that nobody believes that this inmate turned into a bird.

### THE END

*Third Place*

# Somewhere, Kansas
## GORDON BOWERS

EXT. SPACE

*The view is of Earth and the moon with the sun just slipping behind the Earth, leaving the planet dark except for the glow of city lights.*

*Deep Purple's "Space Truckin'" plays as the view slowly zooms in on Earth. It slowly becomes obvious by the pattern of city lights that it is nighttime in North America that we are seeing. The lights of major cities clearly mark their locations. The view continues to zoom in on the northeastern seaboard as the song ends and the DJ begins.*

JIM (V.O.)
*(Very laid back, Man)*
Well, Boston, it's cold and wet out there, downright dreary you could say… so even the weather fits my mood tonight, and the mood of the show. My last one, Man… I've been going on about it for days and you're probably sick of it, but it's finally here and I guess you won't have to listen to this depressing, old man whine about it much more.

*As Jim speaks, the view continues to close in on the northeast, now obviously cloud-covered.*

JIM (cont'd)
I know I've been doing a lot of talking tonight, but when things get final it kinda gets a guy thinking, Man, and I guess it put me in a stream of consciousness mode tonight.

*(JIM chuckles)*

That's maybe getting too deep, But it's the last few minutes of my last show and I think I'm allowed, Man.

*(long pause)*

(reflective)
Do you ever think back on the choices you've made in
life?... When I was a kid, Man, everything was possible,
life was amazing … and then I started making choices.
Back then there were so many options, I could pick and
choose the ones I wanted and just let the rest of them
slide, Man. And look where that gets you. It's like
you've been climbing a tree, heading out on branches and
twigs, and finally you're sitting on the tip of a leaf,
Man, and you can't go forward, and when you  look back,
Man… Whoa! You picked the tree, Man.
(reflective pause)

I guess I picked the wrong tree, and, if I can't go
back, I'm just gonna have to jump.

*The view continues to zoom in towards Boston, through
rain clouds, until city lights appear and the view flies
over downtown Boston toward a tall broadcast antenna on
top of an office building.  The view enters the tip of
the antenna, traveling down copper wire, twisting and
turning, finally exiting into a small radio broadcast
booth, flying past JIM's bearded chin as he talks.*

*The booth is small, really meant for only one occupant.
JIM sits in front of a small control board, one
turntable off to the side is jury-rigged into the board
with cables. A Deep Purple album is spinning on the
turntable with the stylus raised off of it.*

*JIM is sitting in a wheeled office chair, speaking into
an old-school, chromed, broadcast microphone. JIM is
60-ish, tall (at least six feet), medium frame with a
bit of a belly. He has long, graying hair in a ponytail,
a scraggly goatee, and a mustache. He is wearing baggy
cargo shorts and an oversized, multi-colored beach
shirt, with crocs and no socks.*

**JIM** (cont'd)
Now don't worry, old Jim's not gonna do anything stupid,
Man. I'm gonna make like one of them monkeys or lemurs,
and I can see another tree just right over there, and
maybe these old legs got just enough left in them to
make that jump, and then maybe make some better
choices.
(reflective pause)

*JIM flicks a switch and slowly turns a large knob on the
control panel. The Rolling Stones' "Sympathy for the
Devil" fades in.*

**JIM** (cont'd)
The Stones, Man. Now they made a few bad choices,

but they picked a tall tree, Man, and they're still climbing.

*JIM flicks another switch, sits back in the chair and sighs heavily, his arms hang down. He looks exhausted. The Stones play in the background.*

**JIM**
*(to himself)*
Well, Jimmie, better pack up, time to go.

*JIM slaps his knees with both hands a few times before he slowly stands. JIM groans as he stands, stretching his back. As he begins packing his few LPs, microphone, and turntable into their cases, his relief DJ (JACK) enters the booth.*

*JACK is young, about twenty-five, starting out as the overnight DJ. He is tall, lanky, has long, straight hair and lots of tattoos. He is dressed in well-worn jeans and a PHISH t-shirt.*

*The booth is crowded with both men in it and they have to maneuver around each other as JIM packs up and JACK sets up for his show.*

**JACK**
*(genuinely)*
Great show tonight, Jim. I loved the whole tree analogy.

*JIM closes his last case and gets ready to leave. He briefly looks at JACK, a small smile on his face.*

**JIM**
For a change, right?

**JACK**
*(looking and sounding hurt)*
Awe, c'mon Jim, I don't deserve that. You got me this job, and I owe you a lot, but not fake praise! I really mean it. Great show, Man.

**JIM**
*(sheepishly)*
Thanks, Man. It's just my inner demons coming out, I guess.

*There is an awkward silence as JIM stands at the door, ready to leave, his hand on the doorknob.*

**JACK**
*(awkwardly)*
Look, Jim, nobody likes the way the big guy…

**JIM**
(interrupting)
Man, I don't blame 'im. Like Zep said, "It's nobody's
fault but mine."

JIM opens the door and walks out of the booth.

**JIM**
(over his shoulder as the door closes)
Take 'er easy, Jack. Look me up if you ever come out
west.

The Rolling Stones comes up as the camera follows JIM
through an empty office. A man, vacuuming, stops what he
is doing and exchanges a few words with JIM. We only
hear the music. They exchange a biker shake and JIM
continues to the elevators. The scene ends as JIM enters
the elevator and the doors close on him. The music
continues into the next scene.

INT. UNDERGROUND PARKING GARAGE, END OF JIM'S SHIFT

Elevator doors open and JIM steps out into the parking
garage. The garage is all gray concrete and dim
lighting, and is mostly empty. The camera follows JIM
to the end of a row where a late model, short box, 4X4
pick-up is parked. The truck is in pristine shape and
spotless. Expensive but not flashy, it is black with some
chrome, but not too much.

JIM unlocks the truck and carefully places his bags in
the back seat. He gets in, starts the truck, and turns
up the radio as the Stones' song ends.

**RADIO** (V.O.)
(JACK speaking)
Wow! After that I got nothin'. Good luck on that jump,
Jim. This one's for you.
(Led Zeppelin's "Nobody's Fault But Mine" begins to
play)

**JIM**
(Laughing and shaking his head)
You're a real son of a bitch, Jack. A real son of a
bitch.

The camera follows JIM's truck as he backs out, then
drives through the deserted garage and pulls out into
an empty and wet downtown Boston. The camera peels away
from the truck and begins flying over the sleeping city.
Led Zeppelin fades into the sound of falling rain as the
camera nears a large condo building overlooking downtown

Boston.

The camera floats across a wide balcony/terrace and enters an upscale condo through open French doors. The condo interior is very dimly lit. The camera floats through a shadowy, barren looking living room towards the front door. Rain is still audible as we hear a key in the lock and the door opens. We briefly seen JIM by the hallway light as he enters, before he closes the door behind him. He is dressed as he was when we last saw him, but he has been rained on. His clothes and hair are damp. He does not carry any cases.

JIM kicks off his crocs before he closes the door and the condo becomes dark again.

The camera follows JIM as he walks through the condo to the living room where he snaps on a small, gooseneck lamp. The lamp spills a small pool of light on and around an expensive Riga turntable that sits on a shelf in a built-in wall unit that contains thousands of vinyl LPs. The rest of the living room is barely lit by the small lamp, and we see that the walls are bare and the only furniture is a single, modern-style chair in the center of the room facing the wall unit and a large pair of hi-end stereo speakers. Boxes of packed LPs are scattered around the floor.

JIM turns on the stereo amp and turntable, then selects a Doors album from among the shelves. He meticulously, almost ritually, removes the plastic sleeve, then removes the album from the dust sleeve, setting the dust sleeve on the album cover, all the while handling the vinyl only by its edges and center label. He puts the album on the already spinning turntable and lowers the stylus. He turns up the volume and the sound of rain outside merges with the rain and thunder from the beginning of "Riders on the Storm."

JIM picks up a small, carved wooden box and half a bottle of Maker's Mark bourbon from a shelf and drops into the chair, setting the bottle on the floor and the box in his lap as he does so. He opens the box and begins to roll a joint. Again, his movements are calculated and ritualistic, smooth and efficient. He has done this a few times before. A lighter from the box lights the joint and JIM inhales deeply as he sets the box on the floor and picks up the bottle. JIM seems to melt back into the chair as his body relaxes.

**JIM**
(as he exhales a huge cloud)
Oh yeah, baby!

JIM spins the top off the bottle one-handed with his
thumb, the joint in his other hand, and drinks deeply
from the bottle, the top falling onto the floor.
The music comes up as the camera begins to roam around
the gloomy condo. Other than a few moving boxes strewn
about and a sleeping bag in a bedroom, the condo is
empty. The camera finally passes by JIM again on its way
to the French doors and settles on the view of Boston as
the music ends or fades out with the scene.


INT. JIM'S CONDO - 6:45 AM

JIM is walking through the condo, he is wearing the same
clothes from the night before. His hair is nearly pulled
back in a ponytail, his goatee still scraggly. JIM has
obviously finished packing and has moved everything out.
He is going from room to room, double-checking closets,
drawers, etc. for anything he may have missed. JIM
is wearing earbuds plugged into a phone in his shirt
pocket. We hear the radio morning show he is listening
to.

**RADIO D.J.** (V.O.)
(energetic)
Well, Boston, it's a beautiful
morning out there after last night's rain…
(D.J. goes on with typical morning show banter)
(then Boston's "Don't Look Back" plays)

Sunlight streams into the condo as JIM finishes his
walkthrough. Once done, JIM enters the kitchen on his
way to the door and drops a set of keys on the counter
next to a few sheets of legal-sized paper. He begins
to move towards the door again but then pauses for a
moment, deep in thought. Finally he removes his wedding
ring and drops it on the legal paper before leaving the
condo and closing the door.

The camera follows JIM down a couple of flights of
exterior stairs, we continue to hear Boston in the
background. JIM emerges from the stairs into a parking
lot bathed in bright, morning sunlight under deep, blue
skies, his truck is parked along the curb with a large,
dial-axle U-Haul trailer hooked to it. JIM walks around
the truck and trailer, checking the tires, the trailer's
doors and lock, and the hitch, before getting into
the truck. A large, well-worn duffel bag sits on the
back seat along with the cases JIM took from the radio
station the previous night.

JIM removes the earbuds and the radio stops for a moment

before he starts the truck and turns the volume up on the stereo. "Don't Look Back" drowns out everything as JIM dons a pair of expensive-looking sunglasses and pulls out the parking lot, headed west out of Boston.

EXT. U.S. HWY 20, WESTERN M.A. - 9:30 AM

The camera is above and behind JIM's truck, following him as he drives through western Massachusetts on Hwy. 20. The camera swoops down upon the truck and enters the back of the cab, the view is now the back of JIM's head and shoulders and the view out the windshield. "Don't Look Back" continues to play while JIM tokes on a roach held in a roach clip. A feather dangles from the clip by a short leather thong. Through the windshield we see "Welcome to Springfield" and "US Hwy 20" signs. The music continues through the next scene.

INT. TRUCK CAB - 11:00 AM

Same interior shot of JIM driving. The roach clip is attached to the passenger visor, a dark-brown stain on the visor indicates it is usually kept there. Through the windshield we see a "Welcome to New York State" sign. JIM takes a swig from a pocket flask then replaces it in the console. "Don't Look Back" fades out as the scene ends.

INT. TRUCK CAB - 12:30 PM

Same interior shot of JIM driving. Scene begins at the end of a weather report on the radio.

**RADIO** (V.O.)
… and that's the weather. So it's a beautiful day here in Albany and northeast New York.
(Red Rider's "Lunatic Fringe" begins playing)

JIM turns up the volume as the music begins. Through the windshield we see a mileage sign to "Syracuse, NY 86 miles." Farms or sparse residences line the highway. JIM is following and catching up to a semi with an enclosed trailer. The semi suddenly brakes hard and immediately jumps up off the road as if it has run over something big. JIM reacts by braking hard, the anti-lock systems groan as the truck slows.

**JIM**
Holy fuck!

The tractor trailer jackknifes, flips onto the passenger side and then slides crosswise down the highway before

coming to a stop, blocking both west bound lanes. The
nose of the tractor rests in the median ditch while
the back of the trailer rests in the other ditch. JIM's
truck stops 20-30 feet from the semi. The camera follows
JIM as he leaps from his truck and jogs toward the
overturned tractor. Red Rider fades out as JIM leaves
his truck.

JIM stands beside the overturned cab, facing the
destroyed undercarriage. The front wheels sit at odd
angles, the axle broken, and the transmission and drive
shaft are torn up. JIM looks up to where the driver's
door is, looking for a way to climb up the underside of
the truck.

JIM
(shouting, concerned)
Hey, Man!... Hey! Are you alright in there?

The camera follows JIM as he works his way around the
nose of the tractor in the ditch. The bumper and lower
portion of the grill are caved in and the fiberglass
cowling and fenders are shattered. JIM looks in the
windshield and sees the driver suspended by his seat
belt and beginning to stir. Airbags hang limp from the
steering wheel and the door panels.

JIM
(banging on the windshield)
Hey, Man, are you alright?
(still banging)
Hey!

There is still no response from the DRIVER and JIM
rushes to the front of the tractor and begins to climb
the destroyed grill. The camera zooms out and flies up
to show the entire accident scene. Westbound traffic is
backed up and some people are beginning to gather near
JIM's truck. A couple of men are approaching the tractor
as JIM scrambles onto the side of the hood and works his
way toward the DRIVER's door on the broken fiberglass.
Eastbound traffic has slowed as drivers rubberneck, and
it is beginning to back up.

JIM
(shouting)
Hang on man, I'm coming.

The camera zooms in and looks down on JIM as he reaches
the DRIVER's door and looks down into the cab. The
DRIVER is now moving and trying to get out of the seat
belt. JIM lifts the door open.

**JIM**
Are you alright?

**DRIVER**
(voice shaky, fumbling to get out of seat belt)
You see that thing?

**JIM**
What thing?

**DRIVER**
(incredulous)
What I hit! Jesus, it was big. It's gotta still be there.

**JIM**
I don't know what you hit, Man, but it's still not anywhere. Let's get you out of there first and then we can figure out what happened. Whatever it was really fucked up your truck, Man.

JIM and the DRIVER work together to get the DRIVER up and out of the cab. The DRIVER is only shaken up. A couple of other drivers on the ground help JIM and the DRIVER down from the cab.

A small crowd has gathered 15 to 20 feet from the semi by the time JIM and the DRIVER climb from the cab. Snippets of conversation can be overhead.

**CROWD**
Did you see what happened?

All I saw was the back of that black pickup.

My wife lost it when we came around that last corner.

JIM and the DRIVER stand below the driver's door examining the underside of the tractor. The DRIVER is pale and beginning to shake a little. The DRIVER is shorter than JIM, and stocky, with a trucker's gut. The DRIVER turns around and looks back, down the highway. Finally he points to a spot about 200 feet behind JIM's truck on the north side of the road, his hand visibly shaking.

**DRIVER**
(voice is weak and confused)
It came right outta them trees back there, like it was flyin' or somethin'.
(turns back to his rig)
It makes no sen you din' see it.

*(gestures to the underside of his truck)*
I mean, look what it's done. It was plumbhuge! You musta
seen somethin'!

**JIM**
*(shaking his head)*
I sure didn't see it, Man. All I saw was your rig jump
up like it ran over something. Then you went sideways
and I was trying to save my own bacon.

*JIM and the DRIVER walk to the front of the truck as
sirens become audible, approaching from far off. The
driver inspects the front of the truck, running his hand
along the grill and bumper, a puzzled expression on his
face.*

**DRIVER**
There ain't nothing. No hair, no skin, no blood! It's
like I hit some invisible boulder or somethin'! I just
can't see what coulda done somethin' like this.

*The camera flies up, showing the entire area around the
accident scene as two state police cars arrive. In
addition to the stopped and slowed traffic, we also see a
house about 100 yards north of the highway and 100 yards
behind the accident.*

*DISSOLVE*

*EXT. US HWY 20, EASTERN NY STATE - EARLY EVENING*

*View is of the same location as previous but there is
no accident scene. It is very early evening and there
is normal traffic flow. A car pulls off the highway and
drives up the long gravel drive toward the house that we
saw prior to the dissolve.*

*The camera floats down the house, ducking into the shrubs
at the front of the house under a large picture window.
The camera peers through the window into an unoccupied
living room before it slowly moves around the house,
away from the garage. The camera pauses occasionally to
peer into other windows.*

*As the camera begins to round the back corner of the
house, it sees a young girl (SARAH), 10 years old,
running toward the house. SARAH is carrying a beach sand
pail, covering the top with a piece of cardboard. The
camera pulls back around the corner a little, when it
sees SARAH and watches her from behind a shrub as she
runs into the house, the screen door slamming behind
her.*

**SARAH** (O.C.)
*(excitedly)*
Mama, Mama, look what I caught in the garden!

**WOMAN** (O.C.)
It's dinner time, Sarah. Go wash up.

*The voices come through the screen door and open windows. The camera eases around the corner and approaches the door as the conversation continues.*

**SARAH** (O.C.)
It's a frog, Mama. Look!

**WOMAN** (O.C.)
*(grossed out)*
Eww! In that case, wash twice. Your father just pulled in and he will want to eat right away.

**SARAH** (O.C.)
*(disappointed)*
Awe! I want to show Daddy.

**WOMAN** (O.C.)
We will look after dinner, Sweetie. Now scoot and wash up.

*The camera eases along the back of the house and peers into the kitchen through the screen door as SARAH races out the kitchen. We can now hear a radio playing music low in the background as the camera approaches the door. The WOMAN is rushing around getting dinner on the table.*

*The WOMAN is about 35, 5'9", light-brown hair, attractive, perhaps even sexy in skinny capri pants and blouse. She has a very "Laura Petri" look going on. Also has an apron tied snugly around her waist.*

**WOMAN**
*(raising her voice to reach upstairs)*
Donald… go wash up for dinner with your sister. Your father is home.

*HUSBAND enters the kitchen through a door to the garage. HUSBAND is 40ish, 6', blonde,  wearing dressy Dockers, dress shirt, tie, and sport coat. He is carrying a classic two latch, hard-sided briefcase in one hand, and two plastic grocery bags in the other. HUSBAND sets his briefcase on the floor and the groceries on the counter and then embraces WOMAN.*

**HUSBAND**
*(kissing WOMAN and squeezing her ass)*

Hey, Baby. Daddy's home.

**WOMAN**
*(giggles and slaps his hand away)*
Jerry, stop!

**HUSBAND**
The stop button's broke, but maybe we can pause 'til
lights out.

**WOMAN**
*(giggling harder)*
Okay, pause. What happened to you today?
*(her arms around his waist, leaning back, blushing)*

**HUSBAND**
*(holding her the same way)*
You happened. A long time ago. I was just thinking about
that first night at the lake…

*SARAH and DONALD race down the stairs and into the
kitchen. DONALD is about 8 years old. HUSBAND and WOMAN
break their embrace.*

**SARAH & DONALD**
*(simultaneously as they hug their father)*
Daddy, daddy, daddy!

**WOMAN**
*(herding the children to the table)*
Sit, sit. Dinner's ready.
*(laughing)*

*As Metallica's "Enter Sandman" begins playing on the
radio, WOMAN turns the radio down a little before she
sits at the end of the table with her back to the screen
door. The children sit across from each other. SARAH
chatters about the frog she found in the garden.*

*HUSBAND is about to sit at the far end of the table when
he glances at the screen door. The camera pulls back
away from the door, back into the shrubs so that it is
no longer looking into the kitchen.*

**HUSBAND** (O.C.)
*(accusingly)*
Is that Davis' dog again?
*(his voice gets louder as he moves to the door)*
I swear, that animal will destroy the garden if he
doesn't keep it locked up!

*The screen door opens and we see HUSBAND's legs step
out. The camera leaps up at HUSBAND, knocking him onto*

his back on the kitchen floor. We hear SARAH, DONALD and
WOMAN screaming and chairs scraping back and falling
over. The camera flashes to a look of terror on HUSBAND's
face, and then to a gaping wound in his chest. "Enter
Sandman" becomes louder, drowning out all other sounds.

The camera turns toward WOMAN, silently screaming,
facing the camera with her arms spread wide, shielding
her children who are running away. The camera leaps at
WOMAN who falls backwards as her husband did, then the
camera moves quickly into the living room where DONALD's
body flies across the room, leaving a bloody smear where
it strikes the wall.

The scene is chaotic, but not graphic, not showing the
wounds being inflicted, only the aftermath.

The camera now moves back through the kitchen, swinging
back and forth as if trying to pick up a scent, the
music raging now. We see blood on the kitchen floor and
walls as the camera moves to the stairs, searching.
Finally the camera finds SARAH upstairs in her bedroom
closet, crouched in the corner, screaming. The camera
lunges at SARAH. The scene goes black and the music ends
suddenly.


INT. KITCHEN - MIDDAY

**RADIO** (V.O.)
(playing low)
Donovan's "Sunshine Superman"

The scene opens black with the radio in the background.
Then we see the kitchen as if through the opening eyes
of something laying on the kitchen floor (as in shutters
opening). Sunshine pours through the windows and we
see WOMAN's legs sticking out from behind a couple of
overturned chairs. There is a lot of blood on the floor,
walls and cabinets. A large frog hops a couple of times
near WOMAN's legs.

The camera's view suddenly jerks up and swings left and
then right, tilting a little as if it were a dog that
has heard or sensed something. The camera moves into the
living room, whose windows are shaded by trees outside,
and we see a glow outside the windows, moving away from
the garage. The camera moves back through the kitchen to
the screen door that is hanging by one hinge. The view
peers out the back door toward the corner of the house.
The shrub at the back corner of the house begins to be
illuminated by a glow from around the corner.

The camera view turns suddenly and bounds through the kitchen and living room, obliterating the closed front door as it exits the house. A loud, nerve-shattering wail sounds as the view bounds across the front lawn toward a line of tall pines. We can no longer hear the radio. The camera streaks through the pine trees and down an embankment toward a highway.

As the camera view reaches the highway it is instantly jarred, and tumbles. We hear sounds of a collision, wrenching metal and shattering fiberglass. We see tumbling views of semi-wheels and the underside of a semi-tractor trailer.

The camera flies up to look down on the accident scene. It is late afternoon, a wrecker is just now towing the semi-tractor away. A trooper is directing traffic as it moves slowly around the wrecker. The view zooms down toward JIM's truck and trailer parked on the shoulder of the highway behind a state trooper's cruiser. TROOPER is talking with JIM in front of the cruiser.

**TROOPER**
… and you have our number, Mr. Travers. If you think of anything else, please be sure to call.

**JIM**
(sincerely)
I will, Man. I am sorry I couldn't help you more, but I didn't see anything. I don't know how it could be, it's just like there was nothing there.

**TROOPER**
(almost consoling)
You have been very helpful, Mr. Travers. Thank you for sticking around, and be safe, Sir.

**JIM**
(turning toward his truck)
I will. Thanks, Man.

The camera follows JIM back to his truck. As he reaches the door he sees a figure standing on top of the embankment about 100 yards back of his truck. The figure appears tall and to be wearing odd looking clothes, but the individual is hard to make out at that distance. Long, straight hair falls over the individual's shoulders and down its chest. The sun, low in the west, shined directly on the figure, causing its light-colored hair to almost glow. It appears that the individual is staring at JIM, and JIM ponders this for several seconds.

**JIM**
(looks confused, shakes off the heebie-jeebies)
That's fucked up, Man.
(he climbs into his truck)

JIM shuts the door and checks his mirrors, then double-checks them when he sees that the figure is gone from the embankment.

**JIM**
(wrinkling his brow)
That really is fucked up, Man.

JIM starts the truck and turns up the radio. Golden Earring's "Twilight Zone" plays loud as he heads west. JIM checks his mirrors for troopers before lighting a roach. The camera pulls up and away from the truck. JIM drives away from the camera as the scene ends.

INT. CHEAP MOTEL ROOM - LATE EVENING

The motel room is small and dingy. The carpet is worn, faucets drip, there is a gaudily-colored spread on the bed with large, reproduction artwork screwed to the wall above the bed. The T.V. is on in the background. JIM is half-watching the Buffalo late local news as he lays on the bed, thumbing through the contact list on his phone. JIM is wearing only sweatpants, we see a few tattoos, pot leaf, peace sign, etc. A bottle of bourbon and a half-full glass are on the night stand beside an ashtray with a half-burned joint. There is a breaking news story on the T.V. about a horrific murder of a family near Albany. Not much information has been released yet, but officials are horrified by the brutality and violence. JIM glances from his phone to watch the news story.

**JIM**
(raising his eyebrows and muttering)
Humph! I must have driven right past that.

JIM looks back to his phone. "SHARRON" is the highlighted contact. JIM stares a long time at her name, his thumb hovering over the call button.

JIM glances at the clock by the bed that read 11:10 PM, he sets the phone on the nightstand, picks up the glass and takes a long drink. He leans his head back against the headboard, closes his eyes and lets out a heavy sigh.

FLASHBACK
INT. JIM'S CONDO - EVENING

JIM *is standing in the living room, which is fully but sparsely furnished in a modern style. Nothing looks inexpensive. JIM is in his typical shorts and beach shirts and bare feet. He is in a heated conversation with his wife,* SHARRON.

SHARRON *is an attractive, statuesque blonde, 40ish (think Shannon Tweed). She is wearing a professional-looking, above the knee, skirt and two-inch heels. She would look quite professional in most situations, just not right now. Her hair is disheveled, her makeup smeared, and she is crying and very angry. She just found out that* JIM *was caught with his boss's daughter.*

JIM *is standing near his record shelves when* SHARRON *picks up and throws a heavy glass ashtray across the room, narrowly missing both* JIM *and his records. The ashtray leaves a dent in the wall and falls to the thick carpet, unbroken.*

**SHARRON**
*(shouting, face flushed)*
You son of a bitch! You promised, Jimmie, you promised!
*(pacing, waving her arms, sobbing)*
It's the only reason I came back. I can't believe I fell for your bullshit again.

**JIM**
*(moving away from his precious LPs)*
C'mon, Baby, it's really not like...

**SHARRON**
Really not like what, Jimmie? Really not like you slept with the girl? Another "girl" Jimmie? God, I am so stupid!
*(really sobbing now)*

**JIM**
*(moving toward SHARRON, pleading)*
It's not like that, BABY.

**SHARRON**
*(backing away, screaming)*
Stay the FUCK away from me! It's bad enough that you slept with your boss's daughter, but HE caught you…

**SHARRON** (cont'd)
And in HIS bed! You can't tell me it's not like that, BABY, because it's exactly like that. It's exactly like it's always been, except now you have finally lost everything, Jimmie. You blow every cent you make, you've lost your job, probably your career, and now you've lost me! You've got nothing left, Jimmie.

You're just an old, fucked up has-been that can't tell
the truth or pass up pussy to save your life.
*(over her shoulder as she heads for the door)*
Don't bother calling 'til you're gone.
*(leaves the condo, slams the door)*

*JIM stands in the middle of the living room, shell-
shocked, expressionless. He eventually walks to a
cabinet and jerks a bottle of Maker's Mark out and
carries it to his chair, falling into it, arms draped
over the chair's arms. JIM spins the top off the bottle
with his thumb and drinks deeply from the bottle.*

**JIM**
*(sighing softly)*
Fuck!


END FLASHBACK


*The scene is back in JIM's motel room. JIM stares
blankly at the T.V. which is now showing the local
sports. JIM empties the glass.*

**JIM**
*(softly)*
Fuck!

INT. JIM'S TRUCK CAB - MORNING

*Familiar view from behind JIM as he drives on a highway.
There is a large, paper coffee cup in the console cup
holder that JIM drinks from occasionally, in between
tokes off a joint. JIM is listening to the news on the
RADIO. He is wearing different shorts and beach shirt
than the previous day, and his sunglasses.*

**RADIO**
… and police say that the gruesome murders in the
Buffalo suburb last night are too similar to those
near Albany two days ago to be unrelated. However,
authorities in neither jurisdiction are ready to release
details to the public. A spokesman for the New York
State police says that some information may be released
later today or tomorrow. In other news…

*JIM turns the radio off, picks up his phone and thumbs
to SHARRON's name. He looks at the clock, 7:52 AM, sets
the phone down and drives on. A "US Hwy 20" sign and
mileage signs for Ohio (15 miles) and Toledo (159 miles)
flash by as the scene ends.*

INT. JIM'S TRUCK CAB - LATER THAT MORNING

JIM is driving on U.S. 20, his phone in his hand. He taps SHARRON's name and puts the phone in a cradle on the dash. We hear the phone ring three times and the call is disconnected. JIM sighs heavily, taps the redial button. After five rings SHARRON answers.

**SHARRON**
(irritated)
What the fuck do you want, Jimmie? I am super busy.

**JIM**
(defeated)
I'm gone, Baby. You don't have to worry about me anymore, I'm gone. I left yesterday.

**SHARRON**
(incredulous)
No shit?

**JIM**
No shit, Baby. I'm… I'm gone. The papers are on the kitchen counter and the few things you had moved back are in the bedroom closet.

**SHARRON**
(disbelieving)
So, if you're gone, where are you?

**JIM**
I'm not sure, somewhere in Ohio. I was in Buffalo last night.

**SHARRON**
(beginning to believe)
You're really gone?
(pause)
What are you going to do, Jimmie?

**JIM**
There's a thing in California that might turn into some-thing. It's temporary right now, but they said if I can get my shit together it could be long term.

**SHARRON**
(long pause)
(then almost lovingly)
Look, Jimmie, I hope it works out for you. I really do. But … you know you have to make a real change, right? And I've been waiting for that for ten years.

**JIM**
(*severe sarcasm*)
Thanks for that "huge" dose of confidence in me. Not
that you ever really had any.

**SHARRON**
(*hurt*)
That's not fair, Jimmie! If you were being honest you'd
admit I once had more confidence in you than anyone. And
I gave you more chances than you deserved, but I'm not
going to fight with you now. I really do hope you get
your life turned around.
(*long pause*)
Be safe, okay, Jimmie?

**JIM**
(*pauses*)
I will, Babe.

*SHARRON ends the call. JIM drives as if in a trance for
a minute then retrieves his flask from the console. He
opens it and looks at it a long time before emptying
it into the coffee cup. JIM turns on the radio in time
to catch the beginning of Canned Heat's "On the Road
Again." He cranks up the music and lights a roach.*


*Canned Heat plays over the following series of scenes.*

*INT. JIM'S TRUCK CAB - 11:30 AM*

*Familiar view of a highway out of JIM's windshield as
seen from behind JIM. A Toledo, Ohio exit sign flashes
by, JIM is eating a burger as he drives, a fast food
shake sits in the cup holder.*


*INT. JIM'S TRUCK CAB - 1:30 PM*

*Same view as above. JIM driving. We see a "US Hwy 24"
sign and a mileage sign, "Logansport, OH 72, Illinois
border 132."*


*INT. JIM'S TRUCK CAB - 6:00 PM*

*Same view as above. JIM is again eating a fast food meal
as he drives. A mileage sign shows "Peoria, IL 5 miles."*


*INT. JIM'S TRUCK CAB - 8:30 PM*

*Same view as above but it is getting dark. As we see*

a "Welcome to Quincy, illinois" sign the camera backs out of the truck cab, moving up and letting the truck pull away a little until we see the back of the trailer come into view under the orange lights of an exit ramp. As the truck takes the exit, we see that the trailer doors are slightly ajar and a piece of fabric is hanging out from beneath them, flapping in the wind. The camera continues to slow and the truck pulls away into the distance as Canned Heat ends and fades out as the scene ends.

EXT. MOTEL PARKING LOT - 9:15 PM

JIM's truck is parked along a curb across a parking lot from a motel, about 50 feet from the motel and an open room door. The parking lot is not well lit and is mostly empty. JIM is closing the trailer doors.

JIM
(muttering)
Bastards! Breaking shit and fucking with my life.

As JIM closes the doors we see that the latch on the door is partially broken. JIM wraps a chain around the latching mechanism and locks it with a padlock. For good measure he adds two U-shaped bicycle locks.

**JIM**
(still muttering as he admires his work)
Didn't take anything though, did ya? I guess my shit's not good enough for ya. Well, you won't do that again.

The camera follows JIM across the parking lot to the open room door and into the room. The motel is obviously inexpensive by the look of the exterior and interior. The T.V. is tuned to the news on the local Quincy, IL station. The bottle of bourbon and a three quarter full plastic cup are already on the nightstand. JIM stands by the bed, looking down at the liquor, obviously deciding whether he needs a drink or not. He is definitely conflicted about the options. Something catches JIM's ear and he turns up the T.V. volume and sits on the end of the bed to watch it.

**T.V.**
...and recapping our top story, some details have been released concerning the murders near Albany, New York and in a suburb of Buffalo over the past two days. Four are dead near Albany and another six in Buffalo in what authorities are calling grizzly attacks that are likely related. The FBI have been called in, and until they and local authorities agree the time is right, no further details will be released.

Citizens in northern New York State are being advised to keep doors and windows locked and to be wary of strangers.

In weather, we expect more of the same…

*JIM turns down the volume and changes into a pair off sweats, no shirt, and crawls into bed. He surfs the channels until he finds an old movie that he liked and lays back, toking on a joint that he lights, the glass of bourbon in his other hand.*

*INT. JIM'S QUINCY, IL MOTEL ROOM - 2:18 AM*

*The camera is tight on the LED clock on the nightstand. It reads 2:18 AM. The T.V. is the only illumination in the room.*

**JIM** (O.C.)
(*snores loudly*)

*The view pulls back to show JIM passed out on his back on the bed. The bottle on the nightstand is less than half-full.*

*A loud banging and wrenching of metal outside wakes JIM with a start. JIM lays still for a few moments, his eyes open and searching for something, not sure where he is. The sound of rattling chains and the creaking of trailer springs causes JIM to leap out of bed. Wearing only sweats, JIM throws open his room door and rushes across the parking lot toward his truck and trailer.*

*A shadow slips around the back corner of the trailer, moving away from JIM. JIM edges around the trailer, following the shadow, but finds nothing. He circles the truck and trailer, sometimes spinning around to look behind him, but again he finds nothing. Finally JIM drops to his knees and peers under the trailer.*

**JIM**
(*muttering*)
C'mon, Man, where the hell are you?

*When JIM rises to his feet he notices that the trailer doors are unlatched and ajar as much as the lock will allow, a couple of inches at most.*

**JIM**
(*exasperated*)
Damn it! What the hell is it about U-Hauls that everyone wants in?
(*raising his voice, looking around*)

Leave it alone bastards. There's nothin' you want in
there anyway.
(under his breath)
Fuck!

JIM closes the trailer doors and latches them as best
he can, checks the locks, and moves to his truck. JIM
retrieves a mini Louisville Slugger from under his seat
and returns to his room, closing the door on the camera.

EXT. OUTSIDE JIM'S MOTEL ROOM DOOR - 3:00 AM

The view is a tight shot of JIM's motel room door, exact
view that ended the last scene. The door flies open and
JIM rushes out with the bat in his hand. JIM is angry
and it shows on his face. He stops just outside his room
and looks at his truck and trailer.

JIM
C'mon, Man. I just got back to sleep. Stop fucking with
my stuff!

JIM rushes across the parking lot to the back of the
trailer and again finds the doors ajar.

JIM
(looking around)
Where are you bastards?
(leans forward to peer between the doors)
You can't be in there, can you?

As JIM's face nears the crack between the doors, and
speaks the last few words, his breath condenses in small
puffs. JIM shivers involuntarily and moves back a step,
looking shocked and a little puzzled.

JIM
What the fuck?

Now there is no visible breath when he speaks. JIM
again leans toward the slightly open doors then exhales
heavily. A large cloud forms and JIM leaps back.

JIM
(whispering)
Jesus Christ! What the fuck is going on here?

JIM reaches out with his free hand until he can feel
cold air flowing out of the trailer. He moves his hand
around the top and bottom of the doors and feels the
same thing. JIM backs up several feet and looks around,
very worried.

**JIM**
(*speaking into the night*)
I don't know what you're up to, but you leave my shit
alone, Man. You can't get in anyway.

*JIM walks a wide circle around the truck and trailer,
looking around and under, before going back to his room,
again closing the door on the camera.*

There's an image in the minds of many: the prisoner in his cell, standing at the bars, hashing off time on the wall, and sleeping his life away. My days are filled with work as a peer counselor, cooking and eating with friends, maybe a phone call to a loved one, tutoring undergrads at night, and making time for my creative work—I am a happy camper if I can cram in half an hour of pleasure reading before I escape to the dreamland of not-prison. That's one way of not conforming to the stereotype...

Every day, I engage in, and see around me, creative acts of resistance to the system's oppression. My writing is a tangible record of how I've resisted the destructive forces of prison. I refuse to be ground down into the subhuman the system sees me as.

**—Danner Darcleit**

# MEMOIR

*First Place*

# Sophia
## JAMES ANDERSON

I was shackled in restraints, riding in the backseat of an Oregon Department of Corrections (DOC) prisoner transport van lost in thought. I was thinking about how I got here, and I was filled with shame. Four months before, while hallucinating on LSD to the point of psychosis, I had taken the life of a young woman. Up to that point, I had never even been in a fight. When the Judge's gavel fell, I was convicted of murder and going to prison for twenty-five years to life as punishment. I was seventeen years old.

There were three other boys in the van with me that morning. We were headed to Hillcrest, a juvenile offender facility in Salem to pick up another youth bound for prison. Then we'd head south to the juvenile intake center in the basement of the Newport county jail, my final stopping point before prison.

"Anderson!" the transport officer yelled while pulling open the van's sliding door at Hillcrest. "Get your ass out of the van! It's your lucky day."

I felt like I had a pretty good idea of what my future held, and lucky days didn't seem to be part of it. I was terrified.

"ANDERSON, *LET'S GO!*" the officer said again, a little more impatiently—okay, a lot more impatiently. "*OFF THE VAN!*"

"I thought you guys were taking me to the beach," I asked. Newport, where the jail was, was a coastal town. I was attempting to make a joke. "Am I staying here instead?" My sarcasm was a coping mechanism; I was trying to mask the fear I was feeling.

"Oh we're going to the beach alright," he responded. "But your feet won't be touching any sand. We're picking up Downing, and since you're the only one on the van who doesn't have a sex offense, we're chaining her next to you. Like I said, lucky day huh? She just copped ten years on an assault charge. Looks like both you kids have some serious time to serve. Now get out here and stand next to the rear tire."

With cold ankle chains dragging behind me, I shuffled out of the van. After a few minutes, the girl they were there to transport came out of Hillcrest. She was flanked by two guards, and she wore a jumpsuit similar to mine. It was white, oversized, and it had the word "prisoner" emblazoned down one leg in bright orange paint like that of a safety cone. The neon color gave the officers something to aim at when they shot us should we attempt to escape. The jumpsuit wasn't the only thing we had in common. Like me, she had her hands and ankles cuffed, and she had belly chains that wrapped around twice, securing her wrists tightly to her waist.

The whole thing, at least in my mind, felt like a scene in a movie: A tall, beautiful girl, with long flowing brown hair, approaching with purpose as the sun shined behind her and leaves fluttered and danced around her ankles. But in reality, she was just a girl in an oversized jumpsuit trudging towards us. Her cinematic slow motion walk had more to do with the shackles restricting her movement than it did with any Hollywood effects.

For a brief moment though, I managed to forget that I'd be spending the next several decades locked up with men who reeked of piss, musty armpits, and breath that always seemed to smell like tuna fish. These were the smells I'd grown accustomed to during my four-month stay in county jail, and I doubted personal hygiene would improve once I got to prison. Compared to that future, this girl was shining like a dream.

"Downing, this is Anderson," the transport officer said. "You'll be sitting next to him for the trip."

"You're not a *freak*, are you?" she hissed at me as they connected our belly chains together. "Because these pigs got another thing comin' if they think I'm gonna ride next to a sex offending, rapist weirdo for hundreds of miles."

"I *don't* have a *sex*-offense!" I said defensively.

"Sure," she replied. "That's what they *all* say."

Her abrasiveness caught me off guard, and I was at a loss for words. Before she spoke I thought she was just a great-looking girl who seemed completely out of place wearing a prison jumpsuit—which was still entirely true—but her hardened attitude neutralized good looks in a heartbeat.

"He's not a sex-offender, Downing," he said. "Lose the attitude and make nice because we have a long trip ahead of us. By the way, it isn't hundreds of miles; it's only about ninety to Newport."

"See, I told you I wasn't a—" I began to say, before being cut off.

"Anderson, do I need to warn you about keeping your hands to yourself?" The transport officer turned to me and asked.

"No sir."

"Good man. Sounds like we're gonna get along just fine then."

Shackled as I was, keeping my hands to myself was not a problem. Clearly he knew this. I was convinced his warning was meant to keep her from dressing me down further, a diversion tactic for which I was grateful.

After being secured together at the hip, we shimmied our way up and into the van. The experience solidified the notion that my freedom was gone. *Really* gone. The fact that I was bound for prison for longer than I'd been alive was something I struggled to wrap my seventeen year-old mind around. I couldn't understand how I went from being a perfectly normal teen to a convicted murderer. *Murderer.* It didn't seem real, yet I knew it was. I also knew that every minute riding in the van meant I was being taken further away from home. Further from normalcy. Further from anything I had ever hoped to be.

"Alright kids," the officer said. "We're gonna go over a couple rules before we get on the road, First, keep the noise down. Second, if you have to go to the bathroom, hold it 'cause we're not stopping for that shit. Third, if you have any questions, save 'em for the staff we're dropping you off with. They get paid to answer questions, we don't. Everyone understand?" He didn't wait for a response. "Good."

I felt anxious and awkward when I sat next to her, but it was also a distraction from my own thoughts. The anxiety I felt came not just from our terrible situation but also from feeling like she was a twitch or two away from self-imploding. The awkwardness came because each time the van would hit a bump in the road our arms would unintentionally make contact. Whenever this happened we'd both stiffen, and she'd shoot a sideways glance at me as if to say, *"Don't even think about getting fresh, perv!"* I wasn't thinking about it, but I recognized her abrasiveness as an overall mistrust for the opposite sex.

After a few of these glances I tried to scoot further away, but the chains made that impossible. For the most part, we rode toward Newport in silence, but there were a few brief exchanges.

It started when she asked me how much time I was doing. I told her I'd just been sentenced to twenty-five years to life.

"Dude, you haven't even been *alive* that long. How can they give you *that* much time?"

I shrugged. I didn't understand the law, and I was oblivious to sentencing mechanisms. My court appointed lawyer had only met with me a total of three times, and never for more than ten minutes at a time. He failed to counsel me as to what lay ahead.

She prodded further. "Do you have a girlfriend?"

"No."

"Are those other three really sex-offenders?"

"I guess so. That's what he said anyways." I nodded toward the transport officer.

Eventually I asked a question of my own. "How old are you?"

"I'm sixteen," she responded.

"I'm hungry," I continued. "Do you think they're gonna get us breakfast?"

"Nope," she said. "Probably nothing until we get to Newport."

The other boys in the van tried to get in on the conversation several times, usually by blurting out crass statements that didn't warrant her response, or with comments that left them arguing with each other.

"*Dang!* Homegirl's got some long ass hair!" one boy commented.

"Hey ... *psst* ... hey girl!" another boy chimed in a few seconds later. "What's up chica? Do you wanna see my—?"

"—Man, shut up fool!" a third boy interjected before turning his attention to her. "Don't listen to him; he's a dumb ass. Hey, your names Downing right? That's cool, that's cool. That's a pretty name. I bet your first name is even prettier. Maybe when we get to—"

She had finally heard enough.

"—Shut the fuck up you ugly ass, rapist freaks! Don't say anything to me. I don't talk to sex-offenders, and the cop said it himself—all of you guys except him are weirdos ... so *fuck off!*"

The guard driving the van erupted in laughter loud enough for us to hear. His colleague in the passenger seat gave him a disapproving look that clearly called his professionalism into question. Silence ensued. For a while.

After about fifteen minutes, the boys sitting behind us regained their courage and took turns teasing me. They called me lame. A dork. A zit-faced geek. They said I was packin' a tiny weenie, and that I wouldn't know what to do with a girl if I was left alone with one for a thousand years. And worst of all, they told me I was from a family that didn't give even the tiniest of shits that I was going to prison for life. They didn't know me. They didn't know my family. All they knew was that this girl had put them down and it was easier for them to take it out on me than her. I didn't respond to their teasing, but I'll say this: I felt slightly comforted when she leaned over and rubbed her forearm against mine—*purposely* this time. It was a huge moment, and it came unexpected. The message in it was simple: I wasn't alone.

"Don't listen to those rapos," she whispered. "They're just mad 'cause they're all gonna get chemically castrated for being piece of shit freaks! My name's Sophia."

"Mine's James."

When Sophia and I arrived at the Newport intake center, we were separated, strip-searched, handed gray sweatpants, a white t-shirt, socks, and orange flip-flops. Once dressed, we were escorted to an observation cell. We spent the next several hours together, but we hardly interacted. We were each alone with our thoughts. The cell was a square enclosure with heavily scratched Plexiglas walls, two seats, and not much else. It was called the Fish Tank. Sophia and I were the *fish*, so all the other kids crowded around the tank to give us the once over.

The purpose of our stay in Newport's juvenile intake center was to have our intelligence, health, attitude, sense of remorse, and likelihood for rehabilitation assessed in order to determine how we had chosen the wrong path. These "assessments" would be the first entries in my new life journal: a DOC case management file. I'd only be there for a few months before being sent to one of Oregon's many adult penitentiaries, a place where being locked up in a cage all day *was* the rehabilitation.

Sophia and I didn't talk much at first, but when two sack lunches fell through the Fish Tank's tray slot we opened up a bit over dry peanut butter sandwiches and celery sticks. At one point, Sophia told me she was lactose intolerant, and asked if I wanted her carton of milk. I've always loved milk. I quickly said yes. My hope was that it would taste better than the watered down milk they served in the Marion County jail. That stuff was horrible. When I reached for her carton of milk, Sophia pulled it back and said, "So I guess this means we're friends, right James?"

Because we had arrived at the intake center together, we were paired up as study partners for the duration of our stay. Each day, a few dozen youth offenders would sit in a small classroom to complete individual assessments and study packets. Most of the boys disregarded their packets and instead flirted with Sophia. The three from our ride in the van knew better though, and they did everything they could to avoid her. Sophia handled the attention from the new boys just as she had on the transport van—by flinging confidence-shattering obscenities at them—until they left her alone.

In the afternoons, we'd walk in tight circles around a 10' x 10' room appropriately called The Cube. The rules of The Cube required that we be in constant motion, and any form of physical contact meant immediate loss of our recreational privileges. Walking around The Cube was one of the few "recreational privileges" we had. Knowing this, and not wanting to lose the allotted forty-five minutes out of our cells, Sophia and I kept a safe distance between us while we walked. Every few laps or so we'd stop and do a round of push-ups. She could always do more push-ups than I could, and she always took delight in pointing it out to anyone observing. This came to be our daily ritual: laps and push-ups.

We were never alone together. On the occasions that we were outside of our cells, the staff was always a step or two away guiding us through a checklist of behavioral expectations. The staff focused especially on Sophia and me to ensure we didn't get "too close." I understood the scrutiny, but really we were just two terrified kids who happened to form a friendship over similar situations and a carton of milk.

When we weren't doing schoolwork, or walking in The Cube, we were locked in our cells. Oddly enough, they had placed Sophia and me in cells right next to each other at the far end of the top tier. Sometimes at night, when the noise would settle down, I'd hear muffled sobs coming through the air vent that connected her cell with mine. She often cried herself to sleep. I wondered if she heard me doing the same.

Whenever I'd hear her crying, I'd climb on top of my stainless steel sink and talk to her for hours through the vent.

"Sophia," I'd whisper. "Why are you crying?"

She would always answer. Perched atop our sinks, we'd share deep feelings of remorse for the poor choices we both had made. We'd talk about life, and about how it didn't feel like there was light at the end of our tunnels. We even questioned if we deserved to see the light. I look back now with a clear understanding that guilt was consuming us both. We learned fairly quickly that we could lean on each other for support, especially when our family members wouldn't understand, or couldn't understand, the things that we were going through. I couldn't fix her, and she couldn't fix me, but the commonality of our situations provided us each with a small measure of comfort in our new world of clanging cell doors and constant noise.

Whenever it felt like I couldn't hold the sadness inside anymore, I'd tell Sophia how badly I wanted to apologize to my victim, and to my mom, and to the many others that I had disappointed. She often spoke of the many regrets she had, particularly the assault on a fellow teen that earned her the 10-year prison sentence. Sometimes, when all the important topics had been exhausted, we'd fumble around for something of substance to talk about. Sometimes we came up blank ...

"Sophia, my feet are really hurting from standing up here." I'd say.

"I know, mine too." She'd respond. "Do you want to go to sleep?"

"No, do you?"

"No."

Instead, we'd shuffle our awkward positions atop the sink and wait for the other to say something. Sometimes she'd half sing / half hum a tune that I could never recognize, but through the vent it always sounded soothing. I'd close my eyes, rest my ear against the vent, and pretend that I wasn't there. I'm sure she did the same whenever I shared a new piece of poetry I'd written with a smuggled piece of pencil and a scrap of tucked away paper.

Talking through the vents was against the intake center's rules, but we did it almost every night. The bond we formed easily outweighed the minor punishments we faced when caught— losing our after dinner snack, or not being allowed to use the computer lab, for example. Usually we'd be able to hear staff coming ahead of time by the distinct sound of their jangling keys. The noise would send us scrambling off the sinks and into our beds where we'd fake being asleep for a few minutes until the coast was clear. Afterwards, when the sound of their keys faded we'd jump out of bed and resume our conversations.

"James, are you there?"

"Yeah Sophia, I'm here."

We were caught talking only a few times, but it never seemed like that big of a deal.

Those consequences were minimal compared to what we already faced. Collectively, we had at least *thirty-five years* in prison to serve, and neither of us was eligible for time off with good behavior.

After our 120-day assessment periods ended, we were transferred to different adult penitentiaries to begin serving hard time. The letters we wrote to each other kept the fibers of our friendship intact.

My letters to her were written mostly from the cells of segregation units. Upon arriving at prison, I was assigned to live in a cell with a predatory sex-offender. I quickly found myself the object of that person's focus and ended up fighting him repeatedly just to remain unviolated. In prison, "fight or flight" is the basic outline for how conflicts are resolved. Fighting wins you respect amongst peers because it shows bravery. Even if you lose. To take flight, or to walk away from a conflict, earns you scorn from those same peers, as well as the title of coward, I already felt like a coward for the crime that I had committed, and it wasn't a good feeling. Fighting him felt like my only option. The result of standing up for myself meant several six-month stints in 24-hour lock down for disciplinary purposes.

Her letters to me were scribble-scratched from the women's psychiatric ward. She was much younger than the other female prisoners, and they'd taunt and tease her until she had enough and acted out. She explained in her letters that the psych nurses were feeding her a cornucopia of pills. In my opinion, the pills seemed to put her in a fog. I found it difficult to accept that the letters I received were from the Sophia I knew—the girl who seemed to effortlessly outwit nearly everyone in a room. Sometimes, during the rougher moments, her letters would arrive looking like they had been written in hieroglyphics rather than the eloquent missives I came to expect from her. It left me feeling sad. I wanted to help her. I couldn't. All I could do was keep writing with the hope that my words had the power to carry her through the fog.

About four years into our sentences, the seemingly unimaginable happened: we met up again when she was transported to the facility in which I was incarcerated. A new women's prison was being built and, in the meantime, the DOC temporarily turned one of the men's cellblocks at Eastern Oregon Correctional Institution into a housing unit for female prisoners. Even though contact between male and female prisoners was strictly prohibited, every now and then we'd see each other somewhere on the compound and wave. Those few moments of eye contact breathed life into our friendship.

Once, we even found ourselves in the prison visiting room at the same time. After the visiting period had ended, we both said goodbye to our loved ones and retreated to the gender specific exits at opposite ends of the room, as the rules required. Citizens left first. Prisoners were to be strip-searched and then escorted back to their respective units.

But Sophia had other plans. As soon as the guards weren't looking, she smiled, raised her eyebrows, and then quickly raised her shirt up, flashing her breasts at me. She wasn't wearing a bra. I was shocked, much as I was the first day I met her when we were shackled together outside the van at Hillcrest. My eyebrows shot up in sudden surprise, I smiled, and then I noticed one of the guard's bee-lining for Sophia with a pinched look of determination on his face.

Before she had a chance to tuck her blue t-shirt back into her denim jeans, the guard grabbed her by the arm and propelled her out of the room. As she left, the other men applauded. I will never forget the triumphant smile on her face that day, or for that matter, that hers have been the only breasts I've seen in what has now been more than twenty years of incarceration.

One of the men who enjoyed Sophia's "show" was Steve Nelson. Steve had been with Sophia and me in Newport and had been on the receiving end of several of her outbursts. Justifiably so, if I remember correctly. When Sophia was escorted out of the visiting room he said to me, "Hey, that's Sophia! I remember that bitch from the juvenile place in—" I cut him off immediately.

"She's not a bitch, Steve. Don't call her that again."

His comment could have easily been shrugged off as immature and denigrating sexism, but I knew at the same time calling her my friend meant standing up for her integrity.

A few days after the "flashing incident," I received an apology letter in the mail from Sophia. In the letter, she explained thinking it would be a 'nice little treat' in lieu of the fact that I was girlfriend-less, even though she and I were nothing more than friends. She also mentioned that it just seemed like the perfect opportunity to aim a couple of nicely sculpted middle fingers at the DOC. It made me laugh. It made me realize that her stays in the psych ward hadn't robbed her of her feisty spirit.

In my letter back to her, I thanked her for her bravery and told her I respected her efforts at fighting the powers that be with such impressive methods of creativity. Our friendship continued without skipping a beat.

In the years that followed, we wrote letters describing our monotonous routines, our failures, our frustrations, our hopes and dreams. We'd even take turns comparing the petty details of grievances we harbored towards staff and peers. Sometimes, in our letters, we even dared to hope. This was especially true when the state's strict, mandatory-sentence law, Measure 11, went back before the citizens for possible repeal. If the measure was overturned, the state would have remanded us to juvenile court to be resentenced under guidelines that took into account the fact that we were young and therefore capable of change, guidelines that insured we'd get counseling, treatment, and other forms of rehabilitative programming. Our mandatory sentence assumed that decades in an adult penitentiary would be the best way to straighten out an impressionable sixteen and seventeen year old.

For the first time in many years, we allowed ourselves to hope. We vowed to make the most of a second chance if afforded one. The law was not repealed.

Sophia's stay at Eastern Oregon Correctional Institute lasted a year and a half. When construction for the new women's prison was completed, she and the rest of the female prisoners were transferred to its location in Wilsonville to complete the remainder of their sentences.

After ten years, Sophia's sentence was finally up. At twenty-six, she paroled to her hometown of Amity—a word that means friendship. I wondered if I'd be part of an experience she hoped to put behind her. I shouldn't have doubted our friendship though because the letters still came. They were just shorter and filled with different news than before.

After a while, she encouraged me to call her on her new cell phone. It was the first one she'd ever had, and I remember her excitement as she tried to explain just how far technology had come during the ten years she was imprisoned. I was happy for her, but it made me feel alone. It made me feel left behind.

And then we drifted apart. She had her life back: a new job, a new apartment, and the freedom to roam and experience new things. She had most likely found new friends and new ways to tell all the new boys to screw off when they tried to get fresh. I had the same old stuff, the same complaints, the same constricted life.

Our letters got shorter. The time between them got longer. Eventually her phone number changed. Our connection was broken.

Then one night, three years after Sophia's release, I turned on the television in my prison cell and saw her mug shot staring back at me on the evening news. It was obvious that she had been crying when it was taken, and it reminded me of hearing her cry through the cell vents thirteen years before.

The story was breaking news: Sophia had been arrested for accidentally running over four high school kids on Lancaster Drive in front of Chemeketa Community College in Salem. Three of the kids died at the scene and the fourth was in a coma at Salem Regional Hospital. My heart broke for those kids, and it broke for Sophia.

The newswoman reported that Sophia had been seen driving her Chevy Blazer erratically, allegedly under the mind-altering mix of Ativan and alcohol. She also said Sophia appeared "out of it" when officers arrived at the scene, according to the news report.

She concluded the story by stating, "Twenty-nine year old Sophia Downing, a convicted felon with a violent past, is being held in the Marion County Jail facing decades in prison."

What had happened to the young woman so excited to start life fresh and make good for herself? What happened to all those nights we spent talking through the vent about making the most of a second chance? What happened to the vow we both had made to make our families proud again? What happened to proving to everyone that we were more than the sum of the worst two minutes of our lives? Those conversations were real. They were authentic.

Yet, if anyone could understand that terrible things happen while under the influence of powerful drugs, it was me.

Others may define her by her very worst moments, but I believe in her. I believe in the redemptive value of standing by someone's side, particularly during the rougher moments in life. After all, it was *during* one of those rough moments when our friendship was sealed, and I try to always keep that in mind.

After the initial shock of her arrest wore off, I decided to send her some words of hope. I encouraged her to keep her head up, and tried my best to assure her that I'd be by her side no matter what. In this case, it means supporting her through her twenty-five year sentence.

I've been writing her at least once a month for the past six years now. It's not always easy. Her letters still come, and when they do they're penned through the fog of her ever changing medications. I do my best to decipher the words she shares, and then I write her back.

When I do, I always share one of the following quotes with her;

*"Failure is a bruise, not a tattoo."*

And ...

*"There's something beautiful about having the chance to re-write your future."*

These were the words given to me by a close friend during one of my low points, and they gave me hope. Nowadays, my hope is that she sees meaning in them as well, and that she finds the strength to apply that meaning to her own life.

I will never forget her words to me that day in the fish tank at Newport when I reached for the carton of milk she had offered. She held it back and asked, "So I guess this means we're friends, right James?"

"Yes Sophia, we're friends."

*Second Place*

# Limp Grey Fur
## GEORGE T. WILKERSON

"I need a break," I thought as I sat amid a pile of papers, loose pages and scraps that each held a fragment of a thought, a paragraph, a quote. I had accumulated bits and pieces of an idea like someone saving up to buy something, and I figured I might finally have enough for an essay. Or at least a poem. I got off my bunk and stepped out of my corner cell on the tier. Stretching my aching back and standing at the railing, I peered down into the boxy rectangular dayroom and noticed the two terminally ill men on my pod were sitting catercorner in their wheelchairs, facing in opposite directions as if they were about to race past each other. There is nowhere to go in here except in tight little circles, and anyway it was a race neither wanted to win.

I wondered what they were speaking about, I couldn't remember ever seeing them interact at length before. Neither thought much of the other. I noted the way one gestured to a fresh surgical scar on his chest near his right armpit, where a doctor had carved out enough of a thick slab of malignant muscle to feed two people. The other nodded, then pantomimed something being threaded down his throat and into his lungs. He pressed a hand to his chest and breathed in a deep, exaggerated fashion to illustrate a point. The other's head cocked at a severe angle, half-listening half-resting, then gave a slanted nod.

I heard nothing, but nonetheless it made sense to me. Who of the twenty other men on our pod could commiserate with cancer besides them? They'd been wrestling with mysterious health issues for a year, but almost the same day two weeks prior both were diagnosed with Stage Four cancer and granted wheelchairs – they'd be needing them. Right then, their fatigue and breathlessness were still sporadic.

Three months have passed since that isolated incident where I saw Davy and Gary, both about 60 and toothless, bonding in their wheelchairs. Evidently, they'd compared notes, shook hands, and kept it moving. Davy is in the cell to my left. I have to walk past him countless times a day to go anywhere, because everything going on in here is on the other side of him: the cleaning supplies and topfloor janitors closet; the showers; the lone flight of stairs leading down to the dayroom where the phone is, where the pod door is – through which I must exit to reach the rec yard, classes, meals. Gary has a downstairs cell; he's not so in my face. It's about proximity.

Several times each day as I pass Davy's cell I'll greet him or check whether he's going to the next meal and wants me to push him to the chowhall in his wheelchair, which is parked beside the base of the stairs. It's approximately 40 cane-supported shuffles from his cell to the end of the tier, then a 180 pivot right and down sixteen steps, upon each of which he plants first one foot and his cane, then sets the other foot and pauses briefly to balance. He repeats this step by step to the bottom (or top, if he's going the other way). After such a harrowing 70-second journey demanding sweaty concentration, he is tired. For me, it's twenty strides to the stairs, six or seven springy leaps down, and I'm out the pod door in maybe fifteen seconds, tops.

Usually, the "special diets" group is called for chow before us "regular diets," so we generally know we'll be going shortly thereafter. Davy will come on out and slowly make his way to his wheelchair to be ready to roll. After doing his part, he becomes a baton waiting for someone to carry him further. I tend to stay in my cell, wearing black shorts and gray t-shirt – our approved informal attire – until our call. While I attempt to keep my feet and fight to yank on my red jumpsuit (which must be worn anytime we leave the pod) hop-skipping down the tier, sometimes I'll see the empty wheelchair, glance back and discover Davy only beginning his leg, and I'll think, "Dammit Dave, you knew we were about to go to chow." If nobody else is waiting to push it, I'll stand behind his wheelchair, resisting my impatience beneath my poker face and casually buttoning my jumpsuit as the rest of our pod, including Gary, stampedes to the messhall. A couple times, I pretended I hadn't seen him coming and tried to slide out the door, but he called, "GEORGE!" I'm not a very good Christian, but instantly guilt-stricken, I stopped and went back for him. Davy doesn't have to jockey for line-position. I do. Someone at the front will bring him a tray to his table about the time we enter the cafeteria. I'll be at the back, and by the time I sit down with my tray most guys are done eating and the guards are scanning the crowd to see how soon they can clear us out for the next group.

I dislike lounging around the dayroom waiting to go anywhere. I consider it dead time. Wasted. Instead, I stay busy in my cell. I am neurotically productive, reading, studying, writing, exercising – doing something at all times, anything except nothing. Otherwise I get anxious. Sometimes I don't even hear the call, but notice the sudden absence of dayroom noises, and the realization I might miss a meal jolts me out of my head and flings me out of my cell. Maybe Dave likes to wait till the last second too, or was using the toilet, suddenly changed his mind, or it's that his lack of appetite swerved the other way.

Gary is always ready to go. He sits in his wheelchair in his doorway all day; sometimes all night, with a standard-issue navy blue woolen blanket draped across his shoulders and torso like a riding hood. Lately, when it's time for medication call (7,11,3,7,10), he's taken to wheeling within inches of our pod's Plexiglas sally-port door with a goofy expectant grin on as he sits there. He slouches so low, his back is folding into an "N" and his pale face is almost resting in his own lap. It's difficult for me to witness this slowing, sinking, thinning, balding, wheezing process. Despite my being on death row these past 10 ½ years, I've not been around anyone I knew was dying. Of the 150 or so men here when I arrived, eleven have died – twelve, I forgot the suicide – but none on my pod, and the last execution occurred right before I got here.

To be honest, I'm not sure how to take Gary, though I know he's riddled with disease. Big blue- black bruises and ugly black moles appear on his flesh overnight and grow across his arms, chest, stomach. But back before he was formally diagnosed, he kept trying to get medical attention the prison disapproved. He told me how he'd fake or exaggerate symptoms, like walking down the hall to chow appearing ready to pass out, then sinking to the floor when he knew an officer was looking. They'd panic and rush him to the prison E.R. It was a way to take by force the attention he craved.

I hadn't judged him as an attention-whore. When I arrived on death row, he was the second person to speak to me, and came across as sort of creepy like the old man on the "Family Guy" cartoon who keeps inviting his neighbor's teenaged son to his basement for Popsicles. He had a greasy demeanor combined with a soft voice and effeminate mannerisms that made me determine to minimize our interactions. That is, until I discovered we both were sentenced by the same county, and he asked whether I knew some woman. I did; she's my aunt; and his sister's best friend. I sighed inwardly, because I knew my loyalty to family ties would keep me from altogether avoiding him without a real and valid reason. This, in part, is why I accepted his gift—a small bag of tobacco and commissary items—despite knowing the first rule upon entering prison is to never accept "gifts" from strangers; the other part is because I was 25 and quite fit, while he was at least twice my age and out of shape. I would beat him to death if he tried to punk me. However, when a younger, stronger man offered me a similar gift later that day, I refused it, "No thanks." Years later, after we became friends, he asked me, "G, how come when you first got here you accepted Gary's gift but not mine?" I explained the above and added, "But I wasn't sure I could beat your ass." He loves telling that story to everyone. Gary's the only one he hasn't told it to.

To be clear, Gary's never said or done anything out of the way to me, nor have I heard he had to others. For whatever reason, either he kept away from most people, or they kept away from him, and everyone was okay with that. Now that he is legitimately diagnosed with cancer, he flaunts a vindicated attitude that says, "I told you I was dying—but you wouldn't listen." It's true, he'd been saying it. As for his apparent degeneration, I'm unsure how much is contrived. Several weeks ago he "fell" in his cell and was carted to the hospital, where he was isolated in a room without TV access, nobody around to talk with, and no commissary since he has no money with which to purchase any. He begged to come back to death row. Before he fell, he had become a nearly unresponsive recluse, convincing us he could drop dead any second. Upon his return a few days ago, he said, "Man it was empty up there. Even though I don't talk much, I at least like being at the edge of things where I can watch and hear people." He's hardly shut up and appears rejuvenated. His bleak but brief hospital stint secured him a snack bag to supplement his trays, more pain meds, an extra mattress.

Now he's energetic and engaging, lively even, and it makes me hesitant to empathize, because I feel like I am being played at least to some degree. He isn't suffering enough and needs to make up his mind as to whether he's going to be sickly and feeble. If he stays with it, I can work at forgetting he's probably faking some—and who can blame him? For most his life he's been unpopular and kept from entering the inner circle, yet now that our compatriot is back, despite most of us believing only rumors of his death would return, suddenly several guys are doting on him, asking how they can help, what they can do, etc. His snack bag items (peanut butter, Ensure, cheese, saltines) provide bartering currency since we don't typically have access to them, drawing even more attention. "They need me," his benevolent gaze seems to say; his wheelchair feels ornate now, rather than the dilapidated plastic thing it was. He slurps it up like dirty nectar, an unwitting (or clever) social butterfly with skull-patterned wings who decided he loved people after all. Perhaps imminent death empowers one with graciousness.

Every day while Gary was gone, Davy asked after him: He wanted to relocate to Gary's downstairs cell if Gary wasn't returning. But Gary did return, bigger than ever—if forty pounds lighter.

Be that as it may, I see their cancer as a physical silhouette that smooshes these men a little closer to the earth each night, while simultaneously insinuating itself into every thought and inbetween each man's interactions with the rest of us, either elbowing people away like it does for Davy, or putting people in sympathetic headlocks like it does for Gary. Both men have told me they just want to be as comfortable as possible till they die, which is the most they can hope for; if their cancers had been caught a year ago...well, it's too late for thoughts like those. For Gary, pain meds, attention, and donations of coffee, cookies, and candy is enough. I'm still trying to figure out what comfort looks like to Davy.

Davy's skin has turned cartoonish, a Bart Simpson yellow, and his right leg is a caricature of what it was, having ballooned in proportion. I can't remember how many children Davy told me he has, or whether they were boys or girls, but I imagine he would be surprised to see how much he favors that drawing of himself that one of his kids did in first grade. Or perhaps it's my own inexperienced elementary understanding of cancer's ravages seeking to draw conclusions about what I'm feeling and seeing. I am but sketching a barely recognizable outline in two-dimensional space, and clumsily applying thick, waxy primary colors. Although I am a little embarrassed by how inadequate I know I am in the face of something so complex, I am comforted by the fact my attempt to create a likeness of my friends comes from a pure place: I don't want to become indifferent to their suffering, nor forget the beauties and uglies of it.

Most days, Dave simply props himself on his bunk like a neglected teddy bear, hugging a pillow to his abdomen and groaning because a low-grade flame that slow-roasts his nerve endings is barely dulled by morphine. Right now a herniated disc is pinched against my sciatic nerve. If I blow my nose, the spasmodic squeeze of my core muscles grinds the two together to send excruciating waves of reverberating pain rippling down my left leg, as if the nerve is an electric guitar string being plucked. I awoke the other night, still half-asleep, and the pain was so all-consuming I convinced myself I was dead and in hell. Knowing I deserved it reinforced the delusion. The next day when I explained to Davy why he may have heard me hollering at two in the morning, he deadpanned, "Now imagine that all over you all the time." I can't process that much pain. I can't fathom it. The thought alone triggers sensory overload.

Davy has personality. He's one of those people you either love or hate the moment you meet him. He has a no-holds-barred, middle-fingers-in-the-air attitude that is authentic and abrasive. He is five feet tall; he carries himself as if twice that. If you can look past his perpetual asshole persona, you'd find an asshole still. If he doesn't like you, he'll tell you plainly, "I don't like you. Get the hell away from me," in a gravelly voice cigarettes shredded long ago.

I like the guy. Of course, I don't have baby skin either. When I greet him, I say "Hey Little Fella," in a tone I'd use on a five-year-old. It's my way of verbally placing a palm on his forehead while his short arms swing futilely at my body. Pain intensifies his grumpiness, keeps him irritable and snappy. In the medication line, a buddy of mine named Rabbit who's on another pod and hadn't been around Davy in awhile asked him, "Dave, you doing alright?" Dave snarled, "Hell no I ain't alright. I'm dying. What kind of dumbass question is that?" On my way to class, I happened by Rabbit as he headed back to his pod. I looked at his scrunched brow and asked, "What's wrong with you?" After he told me what transpired, I explained, "Well, think about it. He hears that question over and over again. He is in constant pain. I know you meant well, but he's listening to your words, not your heart. All he hears is you asking him a question you already know the answer to: He is not okay, and won't be ever again. The rest of his life is suffering. Period. It only gets worse from here, not better." He nodded, clearly saddened and feeling helpless. His alleged crimes aside, Rabbit's a sensitive soul.

To some people, Gary and Dave are walking corpses stinking up the place, slowing up traffic in the hallways with their wheelchairs, so they dodge away from them, or speed past them through doorways. Others are opportunistic and offer to get their tray for them. Davy told me how one guy would walk to the table carrying a tray in each hand, obviously measuring and weighing each. Dave always got handed the one with the smaller piece of cake. I saw another guy bend down at the serving window and holler in to the guard, "I need to grab a tray for the guy in the wheelchair too," then take both trays to his own table and combine them quickly so he could ditch the empty into the dishpit window before a guard entered our side to monitor the line.

Most guys on our pod try to stay out of Dave's way so as to not make things worse for him, which is the best they can do to help him; and themselves by avoiding his scorching tongue. At least Gary is approachable and will accept a token of compassion—a honey bun, packet of Kool-Aid, conversation—to help ease our collective discomfort of being useless to stop him shriveling into a raisin. It occurred to me I seldom saw Dave call his family anymore, where three months ago I had to beat him to the phone. I realize it's cruel for us to dissociate from Dave, especially considering I'm sure he's trapped in one of those shitty predicaments where we want and need others around, yet can't help shoving them away.

I feel like, as a Christian, I ought to know how to handle someone dying. But I don't. It's like I'm staring at a complicated math problem, and my answer will determine whether I pass or fail—and being half-Korean, I ought to be good at math (but I'm not). So, I asked someone who does know the answer. I prayed.

Last week, seated in a chair in his doorway, Davy was watching our pod's TV, which is mounted high up on a wall across our dayroom. I stepped out of my cell to stretch my aching back, and about then a woman on TV spat in a man's face. Dave cringed and barked, "That's fucking disgusting!" I looked back at him over my left shoulder, and he twisted to direct his attention to me, "Did you see that? I can't stand someone spitting on someone else. It's nasty. I'd rather you slap me than spit on me. I was on a date one time with this girl whose ex-boyfriend popped up. They started arguing and she spit in his face like that. I ended it right there..." he said, his bony finger jabbing toward the memory the TV recalled. I told him about an abusive ex-girlfriend I had. She was a slapper. Knowing I wouldn't hit her back, she liked to slap me when she got angry (or sometimes when horny). Smitten in lust with her, I tolerated it.

This led Dave to share a story about a girlfriend who got mad at him because he didn't get mad at her when she told him she had cheated on him. Which led me to describe the time I got slit from wrist to elbow with a rusty steak knife and had to escape the hospital because my girlfriend jokingly remarked to the intake nurse that I had tried to kill myself for her—prompting the doctor to have guards posted outside my room while a shrink tried to have me committed... We chuckled over the stupid things we did for women, ribbed each other's idiocy. For half an hour, cancer left the room so two guys could have a pissing contest, trying to one-up each other with the most dramatic story inspired by true events.

Was this the answer to my prayer, I wondered. A way to comfort Dave, though we would never physically touch? I thought, I could spend time with him, laugh with him, let him just be one of the guys. For the past week, I've been trying to stage another "unplanned" interaction. Something about it struck me as a tender affectionate gesture — and I winced. It's as if I got a whiff of the desperate neediness his sickness shrouds him in, or it was the reality of his impending death that jabbed a cold finger into my chest. What-ever it was, some primitive part of me flinches against it. I admit, emotional sensitivity has never been my strong point. Intellectually, I am aware of oth-ers' emotional states, but it takes vulnerability to allow oneself to connect to others. Maybe it's that being vulnerable with another man seems too intimate to me, and I equate intimacy with another man as being somewhat danger-ous, since I've only ever really connected with women on an emotional level because I see men as threats. Not to mention I'm in prison, where any sort of tenderness is viewed as weakness, or homosexual in nature. Something is making me retreat.

Back in 2002, when I was 21, my cat got hit by a car. Though it had no visible injuries, clearly it was broken and dead, its abandoned carcass nothing but a lump of plush gray fur. My girlfriend sobbed as I walked over to pick up what to us was our son. As soon as my fingers touched the limp gray fur I had loved petting, they recoiled. Some atavistic component had activated within me. When I tried again to touch it, my fingers bounced off an invisible forcefield I unknowingly erected around myself. It was almost comical how I repeatedly spread my hand out only to have it ricochet to the side before touching my dead cat. I'd curse myself under my breath, "Man the fuck up!" It didn't help. My girlfriend whined, "Baby, we have to get him out of the road!" No shit. But what I said was, "I know, I KNOW—but I can't touch him! I don't know why. Why don't you try?"

"You're supposed to be the man, not me," she shot back. I was willing to leave him lying right there. She nearly slapped me when I suggested it. Eventually I had to poke at Smoky with a stick to maneuver him onto an old blanket which would become his burial clothes. My equally squeamish girlfriend stood by with hands on hips, indignant, as I bundled Smoky up and tied the blanket to the stick's tip, making a bindlestick like cartoon runaways and hoboes laid over a shoulder to transport their few precious belongings, except I carried the thing I was running away from at arm's length in front of me to a spot in the yard where I intended to bury it.

I don't want to merely poke at Dave to maneuver him to a well-worn area in which I can wrap him to make myself more comfortable. But how do I overcome my emotional aversion? I want to be able to touch death with him, help him carry it with bare hands. I want to at least show, "Hey, I'm with you, Bruh. This shit stinks, and it's messy and revulsive, but I'm with you." I don't know if it actually matters to him. We don't speak about our feelings.

I don't know whether it's Dave I'm trying to help, or that I'm being opportunistic by trying to use Dave as a pretext to help myself, to convince myself that I can be selfless, that I'm more compassionate now, that I've changed—that I'm no longer the scared little boy who entered prison and was quick to use his fists to fight his battles, but am now the man of God I claim to be (though definitely no angel) who's quicker to forgive than fight though no less scared sometimes. Like now. Maybe I'm scared to find out I haven't changed all that much.

All I know for sure is that something in me is telling me not to recoil, but to stand still and bear it. Perhaps it's that I know one day I'll die too. Cancer? Heart attack? Execution? Shank? If so, then this is training for me, a way for me to face my own demise and tell myself with confidence and courage: "Okay, George, man up. You've already been through this. It stinks, it's messy and gross. But quit crying and grab this thing with your bare hands. You don't have to flinch. You can stand still and bear it."

There's a certain dignity in that, I think.

## Third Place

# Albert & Me
## DANNER DARCLEIGHT

It is late, the cell block is quiet, and two cells over from me, an old man named Albert gives voice to a noir-ish inner monologue, opening windows on his madhouse of a mind. This is not the first time I've heard him do it, yet it's still unsettling. During my thirteen years behind the wall I've lived near demented screamers who pierce one's inner world like a sharp needle, but Albert is a mumbler, and easy enough, I guess, to ignore. Yet I'm easily distracted, and have a penchant for weirdness.

The content draws me in, delivered as if he were a private eye in a film from the nineteen-forties, and though I only get snippets, what I catch is sometimes worth keeping. Like, just now, he intoned: "...in a fuck-ing boneyard....standing at her grave... with two dollars in my pocket...two crumpled dollars...where'm I gonna get flowers?... That's the thing they don't tell you: [inaudible]." Is he crying?

Technically, I've known Albert for three years, from when he showed up in the orientation group I'm paid twenty-five cents an hour to facilitate. Every other week I try to help acclimate new-arrivals to the harsh environs of Prison F. That's me: field support. Counselor, concierge, consigliere. These groups of ten to twenty newjacks usually range from the fresh-faced eighteen-year-old doing four to eight for a couple of drug sales (his first experience with the criminal justice system), to the middle-aged frequent flier, life-of-crimer, back for his third (or fifth or eighth) stay in the steel-bar hotel. Though, we also get men over sixty—a few every month—who are either doing a few (hard) years or they've been given lights out numbers and are to die in prison. They tend to fall into a few categories: there's the old-timer with mussed, white hair, jaundiced skin, and a mottled, bulbous red nose, doing two to six for his inability to stop driving drunk; a meek, scared old man who vibes "child porn found on my computer"; the one who got a little aggro with a convenience store clerk—when the responding officers discovered he'd done time thirty years ago, they brought him in rather than driving him home; pops who went berserk and shot his wife with a trusty hunting rifle. And there are those who have grown comfortable in an institutional setting, and pull some born-to-lose stickup that earns them bed space in a retirement community where the orderlies carry nightsticks.

That was how Albert presented during the one-on-one I try to have with each man: he said he'd done twenty-five years and had been given another twenty-five. He was in his early sixties then (I glimpsed his ID card), but looked older, and the twenty-five-to-life was a death sentence. If this job has taught me anything worth being called wisdom, it's the same lesson that was learned by the doctor in Camus' The Plague: ending suffering isn't always an option, but one can at least bring compassion to those who suffer.

Though he walked slightly hunched over, with an awkward, jerky gait, Albert was tall and solidly built; bald with light gray hair around the sides extending to lamb chop sideburns, bushy eyebrows, and a good mustache; a chin that looked like it could take a punch or two—combined with the facial hair, this gave him the look of an early-nineteenth-century beat cop as imagined in a steampunk graphic novel. Some shitty jail tats: BIG ALBERT, and blurry words on one forearm; a dagger on the other (meaning he stabbed someone? wanted to give the impression of having stabbed someone?); L-O-V-E written across the fingers of his left hand.

He was favoring his right ear, so I sat on that side and leaned in, asking how I could help. As if to illustrate how powerless I am to address the group's immediate concerns, Albert offhanded, "I've got cancer."

I winced slightly, imagining the years ahead of him, the ravages of chemo. So, as to his dying behind the wall, the only questions were When? and How painful?

His eyes were icy blue. Nice, actually, like shallow ocean water in the color-enhanced ad for a resort. Albert fixed me in his gaze, one eyebrow cocked. This was slightly unnerving at first, but I came to realize Albert communicates in non sequiturs punctuated by that piercing look, while stroking the downturn of his mustache. Pointing to his ear, he said, "They took my hearing aids." Who "they" were was beside the point—guards at the county jail, a prison reception center, or the intake room here—there's no lost-and-found. If something is confiscated, we can pay the postage to have it sent home, but when it's unofficially confiscated ("taxed"), the guard colludes with a sheisty inmate to sell it onto the black market. However, there's no aftermarket for hearing aids—his were destroyed for sport.

As luck would have it, Mr. L—, a smart, compassionate administrator, had walked into the room, as he sometimes does, to schmooze with my boss—a counselor called Ms. D— and keep his finger on the pulse of the inmate population. I explained Albert's plight to Mr. L—, who took down his info, and said he'd get in touch with the medical department. (He did, and six months later, a smiling Albert passed me in the hallway, pointing to his new hearing aids.)

On the third day of orientation, when only two men showed up, Ms. D said we should wrap up the week early, and sent us back to our cells on a hall pass. Tramping down the stairwell, I was behind Albert when he tripped, and fell face-first down the remaining few steps, spilling onto the concrete landing with a sickening thud. He moaned in pain. The young black kid also with us—who had spent the previous two days in group trying to portray what a hard case he was—looked at me, eyes wide.

"Help me pick him up," I told the kid. "Get under his shoulder." We hefted Albert's bulk and sat him on the bottom-most step. Thankfully, a guard heard all this, so when he appeared around the corner, the kid and I didn't have to persuade him that we didn't push Albert down the steps. The guard got on his walkie and called in a medical emergency. Kneeling at Albert's feet, I gingerly lifted his pant leg and saw an obvious fracture above his boot. He was lucky: if not for tightly-laced boots, his ankle could've suffered a more complicated break. Silently, Albert stared straight ahead, likely in shock. There was blood on my hand, so I did an inspection of him, which uncovered a run-of-the-mill cut on his elbow, the result of the fall. I sat next to him, held his wrist and felt a normal, if slightly elevated pulse, then spoke into his ear, telling him they were bringing a stretcher. Jangling keys converged on us, walkies crackling (in a previous life, I would've been one of the techs wheeling in the stretcher, a walkie squawking on my hip). The guard who was with us from the beginning corrected his coworkers who joked that we pushed the old man down the stairs. Perhaps forgetting my place, when a sergeant arrived and took charge of the scene, I volunteered that Albert was hard of hearing and appeared to have fractured his leg above the ankle.

He looked at me, then quickly turned away and hissed, "No shit."

A guard walked me to the hospital where I was allowed the use of an exam room with a sink. As I washed off Albert's blood with strong soap, I heard them carry him past, en route to the X-ray room. Though I wanted to stick around to see how he was, I knew if I asked I'd have my motives questioned before being curtly dismissed, so I returned to my cell.

Allow me to pause before we go any further, and go on record: If you're looking for Tuesdays with Morrie, go to the source, or perhaps Garth Stein's The Art of Racing in the Rain. This isn't a tale of redemption, and Albert doesn't teach me the true meaning of Christmas.

Like most inquisitive casts of mind with their perseverative interests, I make the mistake that others share my curiosity. I set out to learn about

Albert, the enigma who lives six feet away from me, solely because I'm curious. The thing is, I failed, and it's best to let you know that now, so you can cut your losses, should you choose, around the thousand-word mark. This little endeavor taught me that the accrual of personal details doesn't necessarily a person make; and, some surfaces won't reveal what lies beneath, no matter how vigorously they're scratched.

Even though our paths first crossed three years ago, during the orientation group, after his spill on the steps my contact with Albert dwindled to the occasional nod in passing. That changed a few months ago, when I returned from work one afternoon and saw Albert moving into the cell two past mine.

Moving in is usually a complex process as one cleans away the smell and grime of the previous occupant, maneuvers around duffel bags of property, and sets up shop. Popping my head in, I waved to let him know he was amongst friends. I was happy to see that he had a TV to occupy his time (and that I wouldn't have to arrange the purchase of one for him on the black market). Not having much stuff, Albert was already settled in, sitting on an unmade bed, sucking down the final roach-like remnants of a hand-rolled cigarette. A betting man would say that he had done little to no cleaning of the previous occupant's funk. Viking.

Albert said, "Finally made it here."

I gave a thumbs up, and scrammed to my cell, because a guard was approaching, taking his noon count.

"Here" is honor block, a place where the clientele have shown the ability to stay out of trouble (or stay under the radar when they do their dirt); it self-selects for guys who tend to be quieter, more mature, and less prone to violence. We get a few more privileges than the hoi polloi, but for me the real draw is not having to go to the big recreation yard, which is completely paved over, a parking lot mobbed with cutthroats and nogoodniks politicking, selling and consuming drugs, and looking for marks to get got. I imagined—incorrectly—that Albert would also appreciate not having to go out to the big yard, preferring, as I do, the smaller, quieter honor block rec area.

Over lunch, after I told Albert about the different procedures for rec, he said he was thinking of signing out of honor block, and going back to population. I've heard that tune before. Guy gets uprooted from his friends and routine—even if it's for better digs that he requested months earlier—and feels buyer's remorse. That fades as the realization sets in that there is slightly easier time to be done here.

In the rec area that evening, while in a phone booth trying to reach the missus, I watched Albert bumble about, his head cocked in the manner of an intrigued canine. It was just a matter of time before he buttonholed me. Later, as I sat, per my usual, reading on the repurposed auditorium seats, Albert sat down next to me, smelling musty, and of cigarettes. I put away my New Yorker, and ran down some of the basic procedures: when the "go-back" is

144

called, who to see about getting assigned a locker, where the shower room is, which guards to avoid.

"Could really use a cigarette," he said.

"Sorry, man, I don't smoke."

And cue the uncomfortable silence. There was nothing more I could think to tell him, he didn't have any questions or seem to be bubbling over with conversation, and so I toyed with the idea of returning to my reading, but felt it would be a dick move.

I was grateful when meds were called at seven, and he got up to trek to the hospital. By the time he returned, I had managed to connect with my wife. From the phone booth I watched a flock of overtly-religious Christians make a show of giving Albert a bowl of food (the first and last of their alms). They stood watching him eat for a bit, and I thought for their next act they might wash his feet.

Perhaps they would have if he hadn't availed himself of a shower. When he came back, Albert didn't look better or rejuvenated, just old and wet, and as he dried the water from his ears with the small, shitty towel provided by the state, I vowed to buy him a large, plush one from the commissary.

After I got off the phone, one of the proselytizers asked me to speak to Albert about shower etiquette. Time was, the only people not naked in the prison's communal shower were Muslims (religious proscription) and the openly gay or transgendered—never give it away, I guess, makes you look cheap. Now, I'm not sorry to say, we wear boxers when showering next to others.

Ha! I chuckled. As my counterparty yammered, I imagined how scandalized and weirded out the ten or so men must have been when Albert, oblivious, dropped trou, and luxuriated under the hot shower, ass sagging something fierce, scrotum down to his knees.

I knew why I was being asked to intervene—Albert was sitting near me earlier, plus I'm the quiet reader whom people go to with their questions or issues, as if there were a sign above my head advertising therapy for five cents. But every so often I put my foot down, and refuse to play fixer. "Look," I said, "you obviously saw all this go down. You say something."

There was probably more than homophobia behind the beefing about a flagrantly naked Albert. Narcissism runs wild in here, and guys spend beau coup time hitting the weights, drinking protein shakes, shredding up their abs for the mirror and—let's be honest—each other. So, a naked old man's ruined body probably fills them with primal fear: There but for x amount of years go I.

The Old Fart. That well-worn phrase comes to mind several times every evening, when Albert unleashes baritone blasts of flatulence in quick succession, like a novelty closing-whistle at a factory that manufactures whoopee cushions. It's not the type of thing one asks—even someone like me—but I'm curious to know whether that punctuation is an attempt at modesty (limiting the ripping boom), or his savoring and curating a soundscape of farts. There are some that roar to life with shaking, like an ogre awakened. These are big farts, meaty, worthy of note—Spanish-speaking neighbors inevitably exchange amused commentary, using pedo (fart) and cañón (cannon), which I've combined into el cañón del pedo. The fusillade seems to coincide with his return from the hospital—either the meds make him gassy or the walk upstairs jostles something loose.

Alas, Albert's condition is no laughing matter. Hearing aids in each ear; seizures; cancer. He suffers debilitating flare-ups of arthritis during which his back locks up, causing him to walk practically at a ninety-degree angle to the floor. These episodes get him admitted to the prison's hospital for a few nights, and are the reason Albert has a "flats order," meaning medical has communicated to security the need for him to be housed on the first floor, not the fourth, as he is currently. The institutional indifference of an unheeded flats order combined with the lackadaisical medical treatment make Albert's situation sadly typical for all those growing old in prison. Thanks to the eons of time handed out in the nineteen-eighties, nineties, and aughts, the number of men over sixty behind the wall will continue to rise—thus, the so-called graying of America's prison population—as will the cost of housing them, from the average thirty thousand dollars a year to sixty or a hundred thou. They will suffer the insults of growing old in a cold, uncaring environment, victimized by the system and their peers because they often lack living relatives to advocate for them, and their natural defenses are weakened.

Much of one's safety depends on hearing threats before they approach, picking up aural cues from the environment: a guard's jangling keys (so you don't get caught smoking in your cell, or jerking off, both punishable offenses), volatile peers you need to avoid; the heated exchanges that alert one to the possibility of violent goings on; the squeaking sneakers of a fight in progress; a guard's order to put your hands on the wall for a random frisk. Also important: the PA that announces when we're about to be let out for chow or rec; the constant human buzz in the block that signals normalcy and brings mundane but useful information like which guard is working where, what's being served in the mess hall, or a new change of rules that states we can only wear our winter coat outside from October to April. When you're locked in a cell, with a view of five feet in either direction, that steady stream of aural information comprises the knowledge base for that day.

One morning years ago, I watched an old, paranoid man stab a neighbor in the face with a pen because he thought he heard the guy plotting on him all night. The one who got bloodied was indeed up late talking low to a neighbor, but it was because he was distraught, having learned over the phone of his sister's passing.

Scenes like that make me truly feel for Albert, who recently lost one of his hearing aids, and must often feel adrift in here, sitting alone in his own quiet prison, cut off from the larger, noisier one. Always a step behind, perpetually out of the loop. Though, at the same time, there's a slight envy at the ability—by voluntarily taking out a hearing aid—to draw inward, and seal off from the seething madness of the prison, the petty harangues of its inhabitants. I must remind myself to be wary of this voice of retreat, because the right path lies neither in complete solitude as I sometimes pine for, nor in constant contact with my peers, which is often the case now, but someplace in the middle, where I get the nourishing social contact, while not trying to be too much to too many, and losing myself in the process.

There's also work to be done on my passive-aggressive impulse to shut someone out, making them a nonentity in my mind when I get annoyed. Albert drives me to distraction by shaking "clips" (the local term of art for discarded cigarette butts) in an empty can of tobacco, which sounds like pennies being shaken in a coffee can—does it make me doglike if I can't stand it? I had to know why he does this; my neighbor, John, who is a somewhat younger version of Albert, told me Albert shakes the clips to loosen the tar-resonated tobacco, so he can combine and re-roll them into a cigarette.

That recycled cig smells like the remnants of a bonfire the morning after a beach party, after people inevitably peed on the dying embers. As if the resonated tobacco wasn't harsh enough, he rolls with "green thunder," the green, waxy toilet paper wrapper, which, having used a couple times in county, I know is harsher than rolling paper. In between bouts of racking coughs, Albert will toss—unannounced—a small plastic bag to my neighbor, John. But it never reaches. It sits on the walkway, silently asking for help, until I use my broom to move it along, past my cell and onto John, who fills the bag with instant coffee or tobacco, and throws it back to Albert.

Early on, that was all my exclusionary voice needed to think, Have nothing to do with these fleabags, the old man in particular is a bottomless pit of need. As I sat half lotus in the grass outside the honor rec area one afternoon, I looked on as Albert maneuvered around the blacktop, stooping down to pick clips off the ground. I was embarrassed for him, subsisting on what was discarded, as if he were a wino who appeared as a block party died down, and began methodically drinking dead soldiers. Does he notice the odd looks? Would he care?

The general population rec yard is scoured daily for clips by an unofficial cleaning crew of men like Albert. Because, by some unspoken rule, this is not done in honor block, Albert has a monopoly on the territory, and does quite well for himself. Even prison has its haves and have-nots. Albert definitely has not, so I belatedly came to reproach myself for my squeamish elitism.

While Albert would like to work, the administrators won't allow it because his seizures make him a liability in any work area — in their calculating eyes, he's a lawsuit waiting to happen. He's in school, studying for his GED even though he said he took some college decades ago in another state's prison. His mornings are spent in a classroom, for which he is paid seventeen cents an hour, or roughly five dollars every two weeks. Because of court fees, twenty percent is withheld, leaving Albert with four dollars to spend at his fortnightly trip to the commissary. As a comparison, my job earns me fifteen dollars every two weeks—my court surcharges have long since been paid off, so I see the total fifteen—which is supplemented by the largesse of my brother. Unlike Albert, my commissary decisions aren't either/or.

$3.25 buys a pouch of roll-your-own tobacco, yielding roughly thirty cigs. It would be easy and self-congratulatory to say that I quit smoking, and so should Albert. But I acknowledge a gray-area tolerance, and know how hard it is to quit; negating the health risks, and putting on my behavioral-economist hat, I'm apt to think that, for Albert, smoking is a cost-effective way to deal with hunger pains, and will provide more pleasure for his meager dollars than the several candy bars or cookies he could afford otherwise.

$1.50 for a three-ounce bag of off-brand instant coffee. With my temperate caffeine habit of three cups per day, one bag almost lasts the fourteen days until my next commissary buy. Anyone who shells out five bucks for a single morning's caffeine fix will naturally think a buck-fifty for fourteen days' worth of twitch is a hell of a deal, a bargain at thrice the price, but remember that someone like Albert has four dollars to work with.

Maybe he gets a pouch of tobacco ($3.25) and a stamp ($0.46); or two bags of coffee (totaling $3.00) and a pack of vanilla cookies ($0.99). Whichever option he chooses, he'll have to pick butts off the ground. And forget about the toiletries that I use: soap, shampoo, conditioner, deodorant, moisturizer. Albert relies on the one bar of soap provided us every two weeks—it's utilitarian and mildly caustic. Same holds for the toothpaste and toothbrush.

Albert goes to every meal in the mess hall or he goes hungry, but there are meals so gross and submarginal, or palatable yet insubstantial, that Albert certainly goes to bed hungry some nights. Acknowledging all this, I amplify my self-reproach, recalling that, for a time, I'd only give him things by going to his cell, just because I didn't want him to grow accustomed to stopping at mine like a stray cat.

Because such maneuvers, even two cells away, attracted undue attention from the guards—by moving in the opposite direction of those exiting their cells—I learned that I don't mind Albert stopping at my cell, and it's nice to treat him with a bag of coffee one day, a jar of peanut butter the next (remembering my grandfather, who bought food for the homeless rather than dropping a fin at their feet, I draw the line at providing tobacco). Yes, sometimes Albert looks expectantly when I have nothing to give—as my human-engineering savant of a wife would say, intermittent reinforcement is a most powerful tool of behavior modification. But more often, we acknowledge each other, and he shoots me a wink and a pointed finger, like a proper old gent.

In a more free environment, our friends and acquaintances are those who partake of similar activities (sports, bar scene, book club, etc.); our peer group tends to be not much older, or younger, than ourselves. One of the rare nice things about prison is that it allows you intimate access to peers of vastly differently generational cohorts, a more heterogeneous mixture to your contact list. My close friend Whit, now in Prison N, is twenty years older than me (as are several of my close friends here); Doc, before his passing, was thirty years older; when I was in my late twenties, I spent quality time with Marty, a septuagenarian—he turned me on to Granta and The New York Review of Books, I taught him to appreciate "The Simpsons." You can usually find some common ground, and things to talk about.

When I sit next to Albert at chow, he will look up from his tray halfway through the meal, and, apropos of nothing, lodge a complaint. He's thinking about signing out of honor block. The goddamn doctor's giving him the runaround. They had him lying on the blacktop for two hours, stretched out like Superman, because tear gas was fired into the yard to break up a melee. I cut him more slack than I would a younger peer who airs grievances at every opportunity, filling the air with negativity. But the conversation with Albert never goes deeper than those surface complaints.

I can speak to almost anyone, bouncing around, homing in on a topic suitable to share in. Albert's hearing loss makes that hard, though. In those moments, when, for a change, I'm at a loss for words, I realize that part of what facilitates conversation is the construct we create of the other's past life and their current inner world. It's almost as if, with Albert, I mirror those on the autism spectrum who often lack theory of mind, the necessary ability to infer what the other is thinking or feeling. I'm looking and I want to learn, but I get nothing—for me, Albert is a man who walks in the snow without leaving footprints.

Many of my peers are the opposite: they overshare. Using distortions, exaggerations, lies, and psychological reparations, they unpack their creation myths, telling no story in which they're not the hero. The smart money, however, plays it close to the vest. It's easier than worrying that something will somehow be used against you (in county I told a guy where I went to college—he took that one truth, added some lies about me confessing, then tried to cut a deal with the DA). More often, though, you don't talk about the past because it's a sacred space, revisited with care when you're alone, savored, pondered. Someone's convenient recollection of his past is practically meaningless in terms of painting what kind of person you're dealing with at present. Do enough time and your past becomes a different world altogether.

Because it's bad form to ask too many direct questions, I haven't brought Albert into sharper focus. My twenty-five-to-life is for murder, what's his for? He did time in the Midwest—what for? He once mentioned a "partner" who works as a security guard, and sends Albert a few shekels a couple of times a year—what's their relationship? Was Albert ever married? Does he have kids? Did anyone make much of a fuss when he was sentenced? What's his inner world like? He doesn't seem to want friends—or do I misread? Just what in the fuck was going through his mind when he decided that he would be well-served by having "BIG ALBERT" tattooed on his forearm? What are his likes and dislikes? I know he dislikes being teargassed; the four slices of bread given each meal—he likes to eat them with the two pats of margarine we're provided. See? I've got next to nothing.

I'm left to create his past. The early years: Was there a moment of greatness? A game-winning home run? As ugly as it sounds, Albert doesn't strike me as having an exceptional backstory (I've met plenty of men older than he, who, even if they were reserved or standoffish, you could tell they harbored interesting stories and hard-won lessons).

I see him doing physically-demanding work, something on a warehouse dock or in a logging camp. Isolate, the guy at the end of a bar—a dark dive—happy so long as he's got a cold beer and a shot of whiskey; pack of smokes, a view of the TV so he can watch the game. The regulars leave him be, word is he's spent much of his life in the big house. One night, his partner takes the adjoining barstool, and tells Albert about a score. The caper they pull is what lands Albert in here doing twenty-five-to-life. The end.

This character I've created is as cliché as he is flat—any junior editor would send me back to my desk with some heavy notes for rewrite. Perhaps the best I can do is resort to the stratagem of the self-involved, and note the stark differences between us. I have a relatively comfy, well-appointed cell, I have my health (mostly), a loving wife, friends and family who nurture me, a good job, things going on. Albert doesn't. What we have in common is that we're both outcasts, felons, fuckups.

I've been given some insight into the health issues he deals with. Roughly four years ago, a mysterious gastrointestinal condition befell me, triggering allergy-type sensitivities to milk, whey, cheese, chocolate, vinegar, onions, garlic, spicy food, potatoes, tomatoes, eggplants, and a cornucopia more. Doctors, meds, labs, endoscopes—nothing's helped, and I have no answers. This has made me less quick to tune out the commercials served up by Big Pharma, while making me more aware that the soft machine breaks down, it's the lowest common denominator of human existence.

Such thoughts were swirling the other night, when I couldn't fall asleep. I got up and did some yoga in the dark, but stopped for a moment when I saw Albert's bright cell reflected in a cell block window ten feet away. He was sitting on his bed, hunched over, watching TV and smoking a clip that he had to light repeatedly, as if he were toking a joint. I felt my jaw slacken and eyes go glassy as I stared at him, and found myself thinking about Hemingway's short story, "A Clean, Well-Lighted Place."

It's one of the few things I remember reading in college, and I've read it countless times since, inexplicably drawn to the story, feeling a psychological connection. In the story, an old, deaf man sits in a clean, well-lit café late at night drinking brandy. It's narrated in close third-person, favoring "one waiter." The "younger waiter," in a hurry to get home to his wife, forces the old man to leave. The other one says good night to his coworker, but, filled with an existential angst, delays going home, knowing he won't fall asleep until daylight. It's "probably only insomnia," he says to himself. "Many must have."

Like many, I've been the hurried, younger waiter, not fully present. But it was always the older waiter—haunted, kept awake by thoughts of nothingness, of nada y pues nada—with whom I most identified. As I looked upon Albert, I was hit with a simple understanding that felt rather like an epiphany. One day I will be Albert, the old man, asking for another brandy, while the young waiters of the world hurry me along and wish that I'd have the courtesy to just go home and die.

There was a recent conversation between us, so bizarre that, just partaking of it, I felt like Hunter S. Thompson in Las Vegas, drinking his rum punch and huffing ether in the bar at Circus Circus. And now, gathering my thoughts, I'm struck by the similarity to recounting one's dreams for an analyst.

It began, per his usual, with a lament. He took the seat next to me. "Hello," I said.

The cocked-head stare. "I'm thinkin' a signin' outta honor block." There was something in his tone that said this was about more than a light haul of cigarette butts that evening.

"Talk to me, what's up?"

Someone had relayed a message that there was trouble at home. The message was sent from his nephew in another block via someone who locked near us, but there was no follow up, no clarification, and so he wanted to get together with the nephew, which he couldn't do because he was in honor block.

My interest was piqued. Was this an actual blood relation of Albert's, or just the ersatz label one gives to a friend to denote a closer bond than mere friendship? I donned my amateur reporter's hat, and went fishing: "This is your brother's kid, right?"

"My sister."

"Ah, so he's in contact with her, and you..."

"I call, but she won't pick up. It's drivin' me crazy. My sister's the only one I got. If that lousy husband of hers did anything, I'll put him through a fuckin' wall. I picked him up by the throat once, my nephew just stared."

"The husband, is that your nephew's father?"

"No. He's just some guy who married my sister."

The details were coming so fast, but each triggered more questions. Does his sister feel the same for Albert as he does for her? Were they ever close? What's she like?

Albert asked if I knew how he could get into a double bunk cell with his nephew (same six-by-nine cage, but with a metal bunk bed). I told him they might not be allowed to double bunk because of the age difference. Surprise: they were double bunked together two years ago, but got split up after a month because "someone" dropped a note to the block sergeant saying they had a fight. Albert had been admitted to the hospital overnight after an unrelated seizure; when he returned to the cell, his nephew was gone, and a sergeant told Albert that he'd be moving into a single cell that afternoon, on account of "reports" that the two were fighting. This despite Albert's protests that they weren't fighting, and that he'd just like to be double bunked with his nephew.

I said, "So one of the neighbors dropped a slip because you two were fighting?"

"That's the thing," he said, "no one heard."

"You guys have a little scuffle?"

Dig it: Albert was watching a baseball game, and his nephew wanted to change the channel to watch "American Idol." Suddenly, I knew that the young, sunburned schmuck who makes inappropriate faces at Albert across the mess hall is his thirty-something nephew. When Albert wouldn't let him change the channel, the kid swung for Albert's face (Albert said he dodged it, but considering the close quarters, and his reflexes, I silently called bullshit). Somewhat restrained, Albert put his two-hundred-plus pounds behind a punch that "blasted" the kid's chest, sending him back against the rear wall, where he took a seat on the toilet to catch his breath, while Albert finished watching the game. If I were double bunked with the kid, even if I weren't watching anything on TV, I might've punched him on general principle—fuck "American Idol."

"So," I said, "it's safe to assume your nephew is the one who dropped dime, right?" Albert smiled sheepishly.

"Yeah, so even if you sign out of honor block, there's no way they'll allow you to sign into a double bunk with your nephew, not after they had to split up the two of you." Perhaps there was another way. I thought for a few as Albert stared someplace else. "What religion are you?"

"None," Albert said.

(Reader, do you now see the folly of my playing amateur journalist? And yet.)

"None? That's what you told the classification people when you went through reception?"

"Yup," he said.

"How about your nephew?"

"He goes to Protestant services."

Perfect. "I know the Protestant chaplain's inmate clerk — I'll get you added to the call-out, and you can see your nephew a couple nights a week. Sound good?"

Albert was happy then, so I told him it'd take about a month for the change-of-religion paperwork to get processed—a bureaucratic laying on of stamps and signatures that would transform Albert from "none" to Protestant—then he'd be on the call-out. And on the seventh day, I rested.

For the moment, he felt like there was a resolution, so Albert switched gears, and said, "I watched 'Godzilla' today."

I'd heard it playing on several televisions that afternoon, the delightfully ominous soundtrack reverberating throughout the block. Bahhh, bah-bah-bah-bahmmm. As a boy, I'd seen the original Godzilla movies, but never from start to finish (I was more into mecha anime, like "Robotech" and "Voltron"); what Albert described sounded like one of the newer, subpar remakes. No matter, I thought, I can hold my own in more than a few subgenres of nerdery.

And that's how it came to pass that amid a noisy scrum of peers in the rec area, Albert and I parsed the finer points of Godzilla's oeuvre. Albert certainly led this conversation, often recounting a battle in blow-by-blow detail while he telegraphed strikes with either arm. He identified with this big creature who was created by forces beyond his control and just wanted to be left alone. There might have been a tear in Albert's crystalline blue eye as he described Destroyer putting his sharp beak through the chest of Godzilla fils, killing him.

"Wasn't Godzilla's kid called Gadzuki?" I said.

Smiling now, he pointed at me and nodded vigorously. Gadzuki, he said, was no match for Destroyer. But Godzilla got his revenge in the final showdown, when he "fuckin' wrecked that Destroyer."

Having belatedly matured and cultivated a sense of personhood, I've gained a charitable impulse, something engaged in with mindfulness, not simply the conditioned response of dropping coins into a homeless person's cup. The shame is that prison disincentivizes charitable behavior.

If a guard sees me give something to a peer, he'll assume I stole it, and am in the process of selling the item. Giving something to a peer is actually a rule violation—"unauthorized exchange"—and it can earn you a misbehavior report. And were I to walk by a cell whose inhabitant asks me to pass a bowl of food to the guy five cells away—when a guard sees me do it, I'll likely be "burned," not let out of my cell for, say, dinner that night. Poetic justice, the guard will think. The fact is, guards infer the absolute worst about our motivations; they're not always wrong, but they're seldom right.

But it's not just the possibility of punishment that dissuades one from being charitable—there's something darker at work. Even when you're on guard against it, this place hardens you in ways that aren't always pretty. The flip side of resilience can be a callousness to the suffering of your peers, an egotistic pride that thinks, I've learned to adapt, so should everyone else. Note to self: control for that.

When I first started giving things to Albert—peanut butter, coffee, stamps, bread, toilet paper wrapper—he would say, "I don't know when I'm gonna to be able to pay you back." Finally, I had to make clear, once and for all, that these weren't loans. We were standing together in the rec area, and as I began speaking, I was distracted by the memories, throughout the years, of men—accomplished tooters of their own horn—who'd bloviate, preferably when others were around, how they "give from the heart" and they're "not the type of person who expects anything in return," but they invariably do.

"Look," I said to Albert, "don't make anything of it. When I can give you something, I will. Don't sweat it." But my tone was all wrong, it came off hostile—perhaps because I was practically screaming to make myself heard above the din—and Albert looked a tad confused. "Don't sweat it," I repeated, then gripped his shoulder, hoping that would speak for me.

One result of my work as the facilitator of a therapeutic program—not to mention my easygoing nature as I play the Hervé Villechaize of this fucking dive—is brushing up against a lot of people each day. I want to be a person to them, as much as I want them to be a person to me. Because if I'm not, that's when the floor drops away, and I'm in that bad dream I can't wake up from.

What does Albert think of me? I think he likes me, and considers me helpful. If he's the least bit curious, it doesn't show (perhaps curiosity is the luxury of those with enough to eat). Maybe he's as intrigued by me as much as I am by him. Once, he commented that he sees me at night, "makin' that typewriter go crazy"; another time, he said, "Readin' again?" It would be hubristic to assume that he hasn't devoted any mental energy to making sense of me, or pondering the dynamic of our relationship.

Just yesterday, he returned from chow carrying a bowl of apples that someone must have given to him. "Wanna apple?" he said, as he stopped in front of my cell, and held one in his hand for me.

I had a few grotesque thoughts within a second's fraction: That is a shitty, old apple, I can actually see its wrinkles, and I'd prefer one of the half-dozen newer-looking Fuji apples in the bowl; Albert, hunched over, proffering an apple bears uncanny resemblance to the witch in "Snow White and the Seven Dwarfs." Regardless, I took the apple and thanked him.

This made Albert happy. He smiled, nodded once, then went on his way. Even if I didn't eat the apple, Albert was allowed the feeling of doing something nice for his peer, which is a gift in its own right. Neil Young's "Old Man" played in my head. It was one of those moments that rob you of your youth and vanity, leaving something better in their place.

# EXCERPTS

*Full versions of the following pieces can be found
in the contest archives at pen.org/prison-writing*

Everything written in a prison is daring, because as a prisoner you are under the control of others, the struggle is real, the threats are entirely possible. All you can do is hope that the universe and your Creator have different plans for you.

You have the drive to write—then you must.

**—Anna M. Vanderford**

*Honorable Mention, Fiction*

*from*

# The Bizarre Conclusion of Walter Germany

## JOHN CORLEY

One night while Walter was at work, someone broke into his house. Went in through a side window where the dense foliage blocked the avenue in front, Prospect Road at the intersection and DeSoto Street behind. Just as clean as you please, the intruders ripped off the matted screen, broke out the latched window glass, scooted right inside. Didn't steal a thing—wasn't anything worth stealing, not even Walter's old picture tube TV—but the place was torn up pretty bad. They smashed smashables, kicked holes in the sheetrock, turned the furniture upside down. Emptied out the noisy old General Electric fridge and left half-eaten leftovers and smashed beer cans strewn from one wall to the other. Pissed all over the place. And gobs of dirty brown feathers, scattered about from some unknown source.

Walter returned home when his shift was done and found it just like that, vandalized.

His house. His home. His sanctuary. He wouldn't call the cops, though. He hated cops. Cops were the government's hit men. The enemy. He didn't need cops snooping around the place too.

So he bought the gun.

The pistol, a classic faux-pearl-handled Saturday night special .22 revolver, didn't do him any good when a couple of weeks later vandals struck again, squeezing through the same window while he was at work, making a mess of the place, slurping through his food, pissing and scattering feathers, and this time smashing his TV. His little weapon, nestled beneath his mattress, was overlooked.

"I donno what to do," he told Willie the next evening at work. "I got no way to protect my property. I mean, I gotta work, you know? I can't sit around and guard the house all the time."

"Git yersef a dawg," the not-so-closet wino suggested. "Dawgs bark. Crooks don't like dawgs."

"Goddamn black kids, no doubt. I'll betcha any amount o' money it's black kids."

"Sure it's black kids. Who else would it be?"

"Gotta be blacks."

"Could be spics. Lotsa spics live around you, don't they?"

"Yeah, but more blacks. They're all over the place."

"You could always move."

"Yeah, where to, Willie? And with what? Takes money to scratch your balls these days, and mine's been itchin' a long time. I'd like to catch 'em—"

"What would you do, huh? What would you do if you did catch 'em? Give 'em a good tongue-lashin'?"

"I'd do more than that. I catch 'em in my house, I'll shoot the shit out of 'em. Law says I can shoot 'em if they're in my house, and that's what I'll do."

"Jes don't shoot 'em with my gun, alright? It's got numbers on it."

"It's my gun, alright? And so what if it's got numbers on it? You ain't bought it new, that's for sure. Damn thing's so old it prob'ly don't even fire."

"Hell it don't!"

"Broke my goddamn TV, goddamn sonsabitches."

If Walter was irate following the second break-in, he was obsessed following the third. This time the vandals raked long grooves in his sticky, discolored wallpaper, shattered light bulbs, sliced open his couch and snapped off the oven door. Whoever did it spent significant time in the house. A brand new six-pack lay flattened in front of the fridge. Walter's bed was upended, the musty mattress dragged into the living room, and again there were feathers and piss on the floor and countertops.

The gun was safe, though. He'd begun carrying it with him in the truck. After the third break-in, he carried it on himself. And he didn't tell Willie or anyone else he'd been hit again.

Because something had to be done and things might get messy.

The intrusions affected Walter Germany on deep levels. He didn't have a damned thing worth a damned thing in the world, yet unknown hooligans were ransacking what he did have, entering his private residence at will and pissing in the carpet that already smelled like road kill anyway. Ripping up the upholstery. Drinking up the beer. Walter didn't bother anyone; he didn't go into people's houses while they were off trying to make a living cleaning up other people's messes; he didn't ruin property just because he could. No, Walter minded his own business. What was his was his, and everything else belonged to everyone else, and he was okay with that. For the most part. He'd been dealt a certain hand and he had to play it. Which is what others should do. Except, some people cheated.

*Honorable Mention, Fiction*

*from*

# Double Time / Borrowed Time / Time's Up

## ANNA M. VANDERFORD

It all started out simple enough, I was in 6th or 7th grade and my mom thought I was sleeping with her boyfriend. I was. It was such a slow initiation, he was giving me money and I didn't realize the full scope of how it would affect my life and world. When my mom confronted me, and I said yes: instead of being rewarded for the truth, my mom slapped me, called me a slut, and kicked me out of the house. The funny thing about being "poor white trash" is that no tells you that you are. I guess one day you wake up and find out that you are, but by that time it may be too late to do anything about it.

I can't remember exactly HOW I survived the first night as a homeless teenager. I probably didn't sleep. I do remember wandering aimlessly around many inner city blocks. It gets a lot colder outside at night than anyone that hasn't been homeless can imagine.

I do remember feeling ashamed and grimy. At first, I would wait until there was no one around and dig in the dumpster for leftover food. I never had a cat as a pet, but I found I didn't like cats because they became my biggest competition for "dumpster food." I would step on previously smoked cigarette butts and slide them over to myself, saving them up to make something worth smoking. Smoking always made me feel grown and warmer on cold days and nights. At least getting a light was a way to have quick human interaction. Living on the streets there was a whole litany of personal hygiene issues.

I was starting to get a routine down. I would start off in the morning, stopping at a fast food restaurant to use their bathroom to wipe off the "pits, tits, and slits". Thank goodness, my monthly (Aunt Flow) was more like a quarterly event, because that meant spending money at the Salvation Army for the cheapest, most absorbent clothes necessary. Next on the list was to find some grub. Eventually, you see the same people in the same areas. I guess it's like life in general, some are mean and greedy and some nice. There was a nice lady, Crystal, that started saving me snacks and the best trash. "Good Trash" is edible food, anything you can redeem for money or is useful (may keep you warm, dry or healthy—peoples' old antibiotics).

After breakfast and gathering, is the selling and trading, or seeing if anyone has any work so that you can make a little money. Most legitimate businesses can't and won't hire runaway minors and the homeless. We don't have experience, dependable housing, an alarm clock, or anything really.

The best kind of work is the day worker groups: you're not alone, you get picked up and taken out to a rural farm, they tell you what's expected, and usually give you lunch and money at the end of the day. If you do a good job, you'll get picked up by the same employer for as long as the season lasts (like raking up pecans).

The ideal work was in the suburb: shoveling snow, raking and cleaning private yards. What one lady called rotten pears that she wanted off her lawn was the best day in my life. I collected the pears, ate the pears, traded them to my friends, and sold them. The down side was that there was not transportation out there, no lunch, and no repeat work. However, she paid me well for the day, and the pears created a financial windfall that made up for the rest.

In the winter, after a full day's work, one of the worst things to face is trying to find a warm place to sleep. The best place is if you can find a long bus route to stay on. If you have a really good financial week, you could go to the movies, and—it used to be—stay and watch it from the first showing to the last. It would be cheaper and cleaner than some of the seedy motels.

Motels were a real luxury. I did pool my funds with Crystal a couple of times, so we could bathe and sleep safely. When we split a room, we talked and she wondered why I didn't go home. I tried, but it didn't work. I was too grown to be home but too young to really deserve to be on the streets.

*Honorable Mention, Fiction*

*from*

# God's Coins
## MARCOS CELIS

While the adults all sat around the dining room table, drinking coffee and making plans, all of the children sat on the front porch, listening to the oldest child, Whitney, tell a story.

My best friend, Wesley, had been left homeless after a tornado struck and left a path of destruction on the outskirts of town; mostly just power lines, trees, tractors and barbed wire fences, until the tornado made a slight turn that put Wesley's trailer and an abandoned hog farm directly in its path.

Wesley and I sat in back of the group of children, with our backs on the porch railing, solemnly looking out at the sky, filling, once again, with dark ominous clouds. Suddenly, Whitney stopped talking, and, when we turned to see why, we found her penetrating glare being aimed at us both. We immediately gave Whitney our undivided attention.

I did not pay attention to the beginning, so I only caught the end of the story. But according to Whitney, when it rained, it was because God was crying out of frustration because he had so many prayers to answer from around the world. His tears would then form little ponds; throwing his coins into the pond and wishing for an answer to someone's prayer; which explains the constant splashes on the surface of all the little wishing ponds.

One little boy, sitting in the front row of children on the porch, was brave enough to challenge Whitney's story, by stating that if her story were indeed true, there would be coins all over the place. Whitney gave the little boy a solid whack to the side of the head and told him to stop interrupting her, seeing how she had not even finished her story yet. After a long moment of contemplation, Whitney went on to say that the coins, being from God's pocket, would disappear once they sank to the bottom of the ponds.

I breathed a sigh of relief as Whitney's parents, along with the rest of our guests, came out of the house, gathering up their children to leave. Wesley's family stayed with us, since they had nowhere to go.

Wesley and I could not go to sleep that night, and, as we lay in the dark talking, the conversation turned to Whitney's story. Wesley asked if I thought it was true. I told him to just forget that story, because Whitney was dumber than a box of rocks. He agreed that Whitney was indeed dumber than a box of rocks. But the seed was planted and we began to ponder Whitney's story. Eventually, Wesley and I decided that if we could get all of those coins before they sank to the bottom, we could buy Wesley a new house.

Wesley and I put a plan together that would allow us to catch all of God's coins before they could sink to the bottom of the wishing pond. One day, as it rained, Wesley and I watched from the front porch, as a pond quickly formed in a pot hole in the middle of the road. As the rain began to pour even harder, Wesley and I were convinced that coins were indeed splashing into the pond, along with every other pond up and down the road.

The man on Papa's radio said that it might rain all week long. So, Wesley and I lay an old sweater in the pot hole, in hopes of catching us some coins. When the rain stopped, we went to check our trap and found nothing but a drenched sweater with a bunch of mud on the underside.

We were extra nice to Whitney that Sunday at church, in hopes that we would be able to get just a few more details about her story. She told us that we would not be able to catch all of God's coins, because nearly all of God's wishes come true; which also makes the coins disappear, but because our prayers are the reason God makes wishes in the first place, if God is not going to grant your prayer, you will only catch that one coin.

Wesley and I discussed our situation at great length. Our only solution seemed to pray for something. If our prayer was not answered, we could possibly catch one of God's coins, and then we would go from there.

*Honorable Mention, Fiction*

*from*

# The Named and the Nameless

## BURL N. CORBETT

On the next-to-the-last day of his life, Vince donned his best suit and shoes, then crawled to the living room couch to await his death. It hadn't arrived by the time the nurse came, and she shooed him back to bed, minus his shoes. He agreed to loosen his tie a bit, but refused to take off his pants or coat. When Stubby brought Tony for his daily visit, Vince was asleep. As Tony sat on the bed, talking nonsense, Stubby explored the house, tallying his new possessions. After a bit, Vince awoke, pulling Tony, his only child, down next to him. There they lay in each others' arms, two grown men, Tony babbling about the deer that used to feed under the backyard apple trees. Tony admitted to his weeping father how the deer's glowing eyes had scared him at first, but not now. He confided that although they had no names, he loved them anyway, and recalled them fondly. Vince remembered them, too, and he also remembered his wife, Viola. There in the darkened sickroom, they lay together, hugging each other fiercely and remembering those who were gone, the named and the nameless, until Stubby returned.

"Tell Daddy goodbye, Tony," he ordered, tugging him from the bed. "We'll come back again tomorrow."

Tony stood over his silent father, wondering why he didn't stand up. "Good. Bye. Dad. Dy.," he intoned, gazing vacantly around the room.

Dad. Dy. could no longer speak, only mumble phrases no one understood. He heard Tony telling Stubby about the deer, but Stub. By. wasn't interested.

The nurse removed Vince's shoes again that evening, but during the night he managed to slip them on, untied. The next morning, Marie found her brother dressed in style to meet his wife.

At the viewing the night before the funeral, Marie and Tony and Stubby stood by Vince's casket, receiving the many mourners. Tony greeted each one by name and assured them that his father would wake up in heaven to live forever with his mommy and Jesus. The men shook his hand and patted his back; the women hugged him and tried not to cry. Stubby was afforded the benefit of the doubt; appearances were maintained.

During the next-day services, Tony nervously plucked the buttons of his jacket, looking anxiously around the packed room as if he were expecting the imminent arrival of Christ himself.

After the eulogy, I waited outside with Jerry while the immediate family paid their final respects. Then we heard Tony's anguished bellow and knew that the coffin had been closed.

At the cemetery, Marie and Tony sat on folding chairs before the bier. Stubby stood behind them at first, then thought better of it and sat next to Tony, awkwardly putting an arm around Tony's shoulders. He reconsidered that, and simply placed his hands upon his own knees, which jiggled impatiently. Nearly everyone had worried that Tony might create a scene, but he remained oddly calm. Out of sight, out of mind, I mused. God has tempered his pain by granting him a deficiency of imagination coupled with the compassionate gift of obliviousness.

"He'll be expecting Vince to show up every day for the rest of his life," Jerry whispered.

Tony stared blankly at the flower-bedecked coffin, fiddling with his tie.

"That's OK. It'll give him something to look forward to."

Stubby lifted his cuff and glanced at his watch.

"How long go you give him before Stubby sticks him in a home?" Jerry asked. "What with all of the insurance Vince had, it won't cost him a goddamn cent."

I looked to the sky for an omen, perhaps a wheeling hawk or even just a passing crow, but there was none. "Hell, I don't know. How long does it take to probate a will?"

The minister finished his short homily; we dutifully recited the Lord's Prayer. Tony's staccato voice rose above the rest, rising and falling and finally stopping with a two-beats-out-of-sync "A. Men." As we walked to our cars, I saw Marie and Tony collecting single roses from a bouquet atop the coffin. Stubby stared into the distance, bored silly.

*Fielding A. Dawson Prize, Fiction*

*from*

# Rusted
## ANTONIO WILLIAMS

When Richard's friends came over for dinner, they gave her praise on how good the meal was, telling her they hadn't had a meal this good in many years. They joked with Richard, telling him he was a very lucky man to have a wife who cooked this well, not noticing that he barely touched the food on his plate, and, when he did, his knife cut into the chicken a little harder than needed. His words of gratitude were curt, his friends probably taking it as modesty, but Michelle saw the dissatisfaction like a cloud of gnats hanging above his head. His smile never reached both sides of his mouth, and, when he looked Michelle's way, the contemptible glare was clearly visible through the slightest squint of his eyes. And he mentioned spaghetti more than once.

At the end of the night, after everyone left and Michelle was washing the dishes, was when Richard decided to show his appreciation. The slap across the left side of Michelle's face wasn't that hard, but the blow snapped her head back, causing the corner of the overhead cabinet to cut into her right eyebrow.

The meaty impact and the blood trickling down her eye must have held back the second blow that usually followed every first one. But the normal flurry of verbal abuse remained unchecked as Richard told her to get her clumsy ass in the bathroom and clean herself up. She gathered herself, dropping all hope of a peaceful night along with her narrow shoulders, while holding in the rest of her dignity with the same hand that momentarily stopped the blood from running into her eye. Her face composed, eyes unaffected by the sting of betrayal, she headed towards the bathroom.

Bloody tears rolled down her cheeks as she washed her face with a dirty rag. The sink, stained by years of neglect, reflected a distorted image of her face through the murky water. She plunged the rag back into the water and wrung it out; then, she slowly scrubbed her face again. She sullenly thought about the new scab she would be forced to live with for the next few weeks.

The grimy stains between the once white tiles of the floor reminded her of her childhood bathroom. She wore flip flops now, but her skin still crawled at the memory of having to walk barefoot on it. The layer of rust and lime speckles on the faucet and sink handles gave her pause; she always imagined those stains were the blood of women who lived here before.

No, she wasn't alone. She wasn't the only woman to get hit by her husband of ten years. Many women have been humiliated by a man who once told them they were the most precious thing in the world. Others have been swept off their feet by the most charming and lovable man they have ever known, and then knocked off their feet by the fist of that same man.

Michelle knew her situation wasn't unique, so she never questioned it, never thought of ending the marriage. It wasn't like she got hit every day and she knew, sometimes, she did push Richard's buttons intentionally. But, today was different; this time she felt that a line had been crossed.

*Fielding A. Dawson Prize, Drama*

# Univision

## ELIZABETH HAWES

*Physicality is open--director's choice. Presentation*
*can be read or performed by one actor or several. Actor*
*reading "Univision" must be able to roll their R's.*
*After opening paragraph, the scene begins by utilizing a*
*fake remote.*

*With little to no idea what they are actually saying, I*
*watch a lot of Univision, the popular Spanish speaking*
*television channel. I'm a fan because the people tend*
*to be very good looking, with amazing eyebrows and*
*thick 80's hairstyles. They usually seem happier than*
*the commentators on CNN. I appreciate how they roll*
*their "R's" and how passionately they present their*
*information. This past summer, Univision aired the*
*Copa America Centenario, a month-long global soccer*
*tournament. When the United States played against*
*Paraguay, this is what the last half of the match*
*sounded like to me.*
*\*Spoiler Alert, neither team scored during this*
*commentary.*

*[Click on a television remote in the direction of*
*audience.]*

Spanish Spanish Spanish Spanish. Spanishspanish. Span-
ish Spanish Spanish Spanish Spanish Spanish Spanish
Spanish Spanish Spanish Spanish Spanish Spanish Spanish
<u>Bobby Wood</u>, Spanish. Spanish. spanish Spanish, RRRR---
----. Spanish. Spanish Spanish Spanish Spanish Spanish
Spanish Spanish SPANISH! SPANISH! SPANISH! Spanish
Spanish <u>Netflix</u> Spanish Spanish Spanish spanish<u>No</u>
<u>no no</u>spanish Spanish Spanish Spanish RRRR--------.
Spanish Spanish Spanish Spanish Spanish y<u> Rohas, USA y</u>
<u>Paraguay</u> Spanish Spanish Spanish Spanish Spanish Spanish
Spanish!Spanish Spanish Spanish Spanish Spanish <u>Muy bien</u>
spanish Spanish Spanish Spanish Spanish Spanish Spanish?
<u>Si.</u> Spanish Spanish Spanish Spanish Spanish. RRRR--
--- SPANISH SPANISHSPANISH SPANISH - <u>Porque</u>? Spanish
spanish spanishSpanish Spanish Spanish Spanish <u>Foul!</u>

Spanish Spanish Spanish spanish Spanish Spanish spanish
Spanish Spanish <u>Paraguaya</u> Spanish Spanish. Spanish
RRRR----spanish. Span-ish RRRR-----Spanish RRRR-----
. Spanish Spanish <u>Bobby Wood</u>, Spanish Spanish Spanish
<u>quanto</u> Spanish, Spanish Spanish? Spanish. SpanishSpanish
Spanish Spanish. <u>Offside </u>Spanish. <u>Jermaine Jones</u>,
spanish Spanish, RRRR------- Spanish y Spanish Spanish
Spanish <u>momento</u> Spanish Spanish SPANISH! SPANISH!
SPANISH! <u>Jermaine Jones</u>, Spanish, Spanish Spanish <u>Ha </u>
<u>ha ha</u>.Spanish Spanish Spanish <u>aah si</u> spanish <u>ha ha </u>
<u>ha</u>.Spanish Spanish Spanish RRRR--------. Spanish Spanish
Spanish <u>une tiempo</u> Spanish Spanish Spanish Spanish
Spanish Spanish SPANISH SPANISH! SPANISH!Spanish Spanish
... <u>North Americana Jermaine Jones,</u> Spanish Spanish
Spanish <u>Muy bien </u>spanish Spanish <u>si</u>. Spanish Spanish
Spanish Spanish Spanish? <u>Si</u>.Spanish Spanish Spanish
<u>mucho importante</u>.Spanish Spanish. RRRR---- SPANISH
SPANISHSPANISH SPANISH - Spanish Spanish <u>goalas</u> Spanish.
Spanish <u>ha ha ha</u> Spanish Spanish Spanish<u>mucho</u> Spanish
Spanish Spanish Spanish? Spanish Spanish Spanish <u>como </u>
Spanish? Spanish Spanish. SPANISH.SPANISHSPANISH. Span-
ish <u>rapido</u> Spanish - Spanish Spanish. <u>Columbia, Costa </u>
<u>Rica, y Paraguay</u> Spanish Spanish Spanish Spanish Spanish
SpanishRRRR---- Spanish. Spanish <u>an houra</u> Spanish
Spanish - Spanish. Spanish. <u>Clint Dempsey</u>, spanish
Spanish, RRRR-------. Spanish, Spanish <u>Clint Dempsey</u>.
Spanish Spanish Spanish. Spanish Spanish Spanish
SPANISH! SPANISH! SPANISH! Spanish --<u>mmm</u>, Spanish<u> si</u>.
Spanish Spanish Spanish Spanish <u>No importa</u> spanish
Spanish Spanish Spanish RRRR-------- Spanish? <u>No.</u>
Spanish Spanish Spanish Spanish RRRR----SpanishRRRR---
Spanish <u>central </u>Spanish Spanish <u>Victor Ayayla </u>Spanish
Spanish! Spanish! Spanish Spanish Spanish Spanish <u>Ayayla </u>
Spanish <u>uno</u> spanish Spanish Spanish Spanish SPANISH
SPANISH Spanish?<u> Si.</u> Spanish SPANISH SPANISH SPANISH <u>muy</u>
Spanish <u>Jermaine Jones</u>, Spanish Spanish Spanish Spanish,
Spanishspanish. Span-ish<u>Beckerman</u>... Spanish Spanish
Spanish SpanishRRRR---- Spanish Spanish<u>Beckerman</u>.
Spanish Spanish Spanish <u>mucho tiempo</u> Spanish
Spanish<u>ooohh</u>- Spanish Spanish RRRR---,Spanish. <u>Mucho</u>
Spanish, spanish <u>Dempsey</u> Spanish, RRRR-------. Spanish.
Spanish Spanish Spanish Spanish Spanish Spanish <u>Team USA</u>
Spanish SPANISH! SPANISH! SPANISH! Spanish? Spanish <u>si</u>.
Spanish Spanish Spanish spanish<u>seis</u>. <u>No no no</u> spanish
Spanish Spanish Spanish RRRR----- <u>.No biente cinco con</u>
Spanish Spanish, <u>John Brookes</u> Spanish Spanish Spanish y
<u>Brookes</u> Spanish Spanish Spanish Spanish Spanish Spanish!
Spanish!Spanish Spanish Spanish Spanish Spanish <u>Muy bien</u>
spanish Spanish Spanish Spanish Spanish Spanish Spanish?
<u>Si.</u> Spanish Spanish Spanish Spanish Spanish. RRRR----
SPANISH SPANISHSPANISH SPANISH - <u>Porque?</u> Spanish spanish
spanishSpanish Spanish <u>garcias. Buenas Tardes, con </u>
<u>Univision, Miguel Herrara y Juan Avang.</u>

*from*

# SYmantyX
## BENJAMIN FRANDSEN

**NARRATOR**

Coincidence. Is it really only what it seems—two events intersecting in no discernible pattern? All things in nature are made up of patterns. Patterns are formed by series of intersections.People do things because they have the will to do them.The intersections of each of our wills also form patterns. Two chemicals meet and cause a reaction. Two mycelial threads collide and form a mushroom. Two lovers unite and create a child.

The Book of the Samurai says, "It is bad when one thing becomes two." The Bible says, "The twain shall become one." Mark Twain says, "A dream that comes only once is oftenest an idle accident and hasn't any message. But the recurrent dream is quite another matter. Oftener than not, it has come on business."

*INT: JOHN'S APARTMENT, CAMBRIDGE, MASS*
*LIBRA, 20's, sharply dressed, intelligent eyes, strong Irish lilt when she speaks. LIBRA snatches a journal from JOHN, M.I.T. sweatshirt, two day stubble.*

**JOHN**

What the hell? I spent...

**LIBRA**

...all your time in this bloody thing? I know! When you need to be working. Now I know it doesn't come natural for a pisces t'do any actual work. They're dreams, my starry eyed cousin. Everyone has dreams. But they wake up. Whatcha need is a bit o' Doctor Whack. *(smacks his head)* t'knock some sense in you. Your father gave up everything for you, you square headed dolt. So you could wear that cap and gown. And he'll be out in time t'see it. D'you know what that means to him? And what about Lily? Flying out in less than a week to see her distractible prince graduate.

**JOHN**
I'm going to graduate. But I need to find the connection.
*(tapping the journal)* It's in here. I just… have to find
it. The patterns keep surfacing. It means something.

**LIBRA**
And if it doesn't? If it's nought but coincidence? What
then?

**JOHN**
Yesterday? I heard the word 'portentous' three times
in three different places. I haven't heard that word
in years. Three times? Don't you think it has to mean
something?

**LIBRA**
Ay. It does. It means you're not taking your Ritalin,
Mr. A.D.D. You're going to face your dad, tell him you
were too busy playing connect the dots in your damn
dream journal to graduate?


*INT. NSA HEADQUARTERS, FORT MEAD, MARYLAND -*
*Dour senior cryptanalyst Edward BLEVINS (40s) glowers*
*over the shoulder of his subordinate, Amir JAFAR (20s),*
*at a large flat screen monitor.*

**BLEVINS**
When did this come in?

**JAFAR**
The M455MPP flagged the attachment from the email as a
conversation of Interest at 0955 hours. Stutterlogic
filters scanned the text and forwarded it to our
cryptanalysts seventeen minutes ago.


**BLEVINS**
What the hell is it?


**JAFAR**
*(hint of admiration)* Some M.I.T. student. I doubt he
even knows what a game changer this program could be.
*(off Blevins' scowl)*
If it works.


*INT. SCI-TECH FAIR, M.I.T. CAMPUS*
*Richard LUCIAN (40s) dollar signs in his eyes. His*
*tailored, navy suit contrasts with his ghostly skin.*

172

**LUCIAN**

You've created a program that mines and tracks collective consciousness. Do you realize what this could mean to group dynamics? We're a private sector security firm with a high demand for technology capital.

**JOHN**

You mean mercenaries.

**LUCIAN**

We provide specialized services for clients that require … unique talents. And we pay well for it. I think I'd like to buy it.

**JOHN**

Afraid I don't understand.

**LUCIAN**

Come now. Surely you've considered the implications. Tying common threads from separate interviews, interrogations.

*JOHN's mouth puckers like he's tasting a lemon.*

**JOHN**

Wiretaps.

**LUCIAN**

Perhaps. Would that be so bad?

**JOHN**

Yes. I designed it for think tanks, not thought police. You know, you have too many teeth. Anyone ever told you that?

*Lucian flashes another smile, this one laced with menace. He slides a business card into John's shirt pocket and lowers his voice.*

**LUCIAN**

I would think that, with your father's release next week, you'd jump at the chance to show you've made something of yourself.

*John's expression is infused with such cold fury that Lucian's bodyguard moves his bulky frame forward protectively. John is too pissed to care.*

**JOHN**

Who are you? What do you know about me?

My criterion for daring writing:

*I was shaking as I wrote*

*I felt it was super important at the time*

*I felt vulnerable*

*I was conflicted about expressing the message*

*The writing involved things that I had been thinking about for a while but was fearful to put to paper*

**—Elizabeth Hawes**

*Honorable Mention, Drama*

*from*

# The Dystopian Hermit Monk: Poetry & Drama In One Act

## PAUL SWEHLA

(Blackout. Cue: Nystedt's Op. 111, "Stabat Mater."
Enter Lilith, a decidedly goth figure who offers her
breast to Monk. Her movement is contorted, creepy,
over pronounced, writhing with sex and death. Images
appropriate to Monk's following monologue are projected
on the screen: dark, implying sexual abuse of a male
child by a woman, maternal incest, homosexuality, a
snake. Milkweed and monarch butterflies. A wooden bridge
and stream, etc. Peer and Brand take turns miming
appropriate parts as Monk recites the poem.)

**MONK**

The order of Mother Right dominates black times of
youthful milkweed larvae.

Tiresias captivates innocent minds with prophetic
Monarch butterflies.

Serpents slither in the grass by the stream under the
old wooden bridge, whispering how women enjoy sex more
than men.

The priest claims that something evil resides in my
house after I confess that all I really want to do

(Monk and Lilith act out the next stanza)

is suck on the nipple of any Great Mother,
Mary, Astarte, Teresa of Avila, Guadalupe or Asherah;

one of her hands at the base of my neck,
the other with fingers flowing through my hair

Less to do with sex than transfiguration — sleep, peace,
and death —
No intent to blaspheme the Spirit.
But Lilith, she eats me alive, a Mother she is not.
Sucked dry with erotic stealth, there's no reprieve for
the soul.

Steel gray and blue at the backdrop of a black, fringed
treeline in silhouette, mid November,
reminds me of the solitude yet to come with diminished
light,
and shortening of sub-zero days and howling northern
nights.

I no longer resent the Teutons or Celts,
nor the medieval Christians,
for bequeathing us with Yule,
Saturnalia or even Sol Invictus Mithras.

*(Monk slowly lowers to the ground as if dying on his
back. Lilith mounts him and they copulate. Lilith exits
as Monk curls into a fetal position.)*

*(Monk rises in victory to recite the last two stanzas
with fervor.)*

*(Cue: Carl Orff's "O Fortuna", edit accordingly)*

Fire up the log of incest and revelry!
Let Mother give birth to our son.
Fertilize the fish and Easter eggs:
The boy must inseminate Mother and die with the setting
sun.

Oh, to be born again — to come again!
Light of the world, ebb and flow as one.
Winter Solstice, I am your son reborn:
Praise for the day of the Unconquerable sun.

*(Montage fades, lights dim. Curtains.)*

*(Cue: Miles Davis' "Freddie Freeloader." Curtains are
closed and scene changes; voices, laughter, talking,
glasses, plates, silverware. Trumpet solo fades.)*

*Honorable Mention, Drama*

*from*

# The Golden Veneer
## ESSAU A. STRAWBERRY


The posh room has broad lighting, exposed brick, and polished floors. A group of men and women sit in a circle.

A scruffy man, WILLIE (60s) speaks:

**WILLIE**
Every day's a struggle being an elder man… well they have these, these pills, ya know, v-egg-rah. They're for penis erections…

*A vivacious Brazilian with a megawatt smile giggles. This is BRIZA, the local Sex Addicts Anonymous facilitator.*

*Her eyes move from Willie to Paige, who heads into THE KITCHENETTE acknowledging no one.*

*At the sink, she thoroughly washes her hands. Next, she pours a hot cup of coffee. Last, she places the ten bucks into the charity jar, and then she joins the group.*

**WILLIE**
…forty years of marriage having prudish sex with that woman. She's dead; now I get to have anal sex--

*A chair SCREECHES interrupting the group.*
*Paige drags the chair while balancing coffee in the other hand. She inserts the chair between Willie and CHELSEA, a sullen college girl.*

**CHELSEA**
O-M-G.

*Chelsea frets at the lack of personal space.*

**CHELSEA**

Really? I can't even.

*She scoots away.*

### PAIGE
Don't you have a frat party to be raped at or something?

*Willie scoffs.*

### PAIGE
And don't get me started on you, old man.

*She scowls — recovery devotees anticipates Paiges's next insult. Briza defuses the tension—*

### BRIZA
For sharing, thank you, Willie. Welcome to recovery, Paige.

*Her accent is nothing short of sexy.*

### BRIZA
Hola, my name, Briza, and I am recovering from sex addiction. It has been for me 120 days for last relapse behaviors.

**The group:** "Welcome, Briza."

*The room goes quiet—all stare—it's Paige's turn. First, a SIP of coffee, then:*

### PAIGE
Yup, I'm Paige. That is me…

*Loyalty is Paige's strength, Achilles heel: sex. Which doesn't bode well. Her addiction requires constant rehab.*

### PAIGE
…oh, let's see… it's been ten minutes since my last relapse.

*Off their appalled looks:*

### PAIGE
What? A girl's gotta eat.

*Briza's head falls into hands.*

*Honorable Mention, Nonfiction*

*from*

# Solitary Confinement
## BRANTON NOOJIN

This is my 19th year in prison. My eyes hurt from lack of sunlight. It will leave permanent damage even when I am released.

I am permitted one twenty minute phone call per week. It's like a TV program where someone is arrested. All they keep asking is, "Can I have my one phone call?" I've lost nearly all contact with outside civilization, as that one call is reserved for my dear mother.

Our meals come on disposable trays. Usually the food is cold by the time they are placed in our food slots. The trays are not made with enough slots for a balanced meal, so our dessert or bread is often floating in our soup.

If you're not fortunate enough to have loved ones who send you money for food and other needed items from Commissary, you will starve and suffer unfathomable ways. Besides the call, commissary delivery is the sole bright spot in the week. As soon as I hang up I long for next week's call. As soon as Commissary departs, not a day goes by that I'm not waiting for its return.

I haven't had a visit in years. These are allowed – on a TV screen. No sense in having my family drive all day long for that and, at this point, my wish to see them that way is gone.

My mistakes belong to me. I take responsibility for my poor judgment that brought me to prison. Solitary Confinement has designed to break me. It can't, I hope – it didn't make me.

A Concrete Death

I am the nucleus
Of a cube of concrete
I give it life
It feeds on my heartbeat
Life ruined at speed of light
Mc squared equaled me
In the vacuum of the past
Now I'm relativity
Then, I was lost
Now I'm one with my truth
Soul-searching found me
That is lie-detect-proof
Wasn't always on point
Now I'm sharp as a razor
Quid pro quo is my motto
Favor for a favor
Treat all with respect
Those words are my policy
Something for something
Fair exchange, not robbery
I repent, seek forgiveness
And might – no surrender
Life is a bitch
Still I request to friend her
Building my will
And my strength in abundance
Can say no to drugs
Since I'm full of substance
Wealthy in thought
Not poor like my past judgment
Feeling some pride
Knowing I really done this
Yet each day's so hard
Will I live to complete
My soul's mission, or die
In this tomb of concrete?

Update:
Today I emerged from Solitary – alive, but not unscathed.

*Honorable Mention, Nonfiction*

*from*

# Conflagration
## WILLIAM ANDERSON

I'd joined the youth group of a charismatic mega-church. Faith, community, the focus on things larger than myself replaced the alcohol, hallucinogens, and industrial solvent that, in my recent past, robbing my body of oxygen, nearly killed me. When I was asked to join a select group of teenagers on a mission trip to an orphanage Central America, I'd agreed.

We'd been given a morning to meditate and reflect, but with specific instructions to stay within the property of the orphanage: three acres, more than enough room to roam – unless you were me. Beyond the fence that marked the boundary line ran a shallow stream through a ravine. Beneath the palette verde of its tropical canopy, leaves rustling, branches cracking beneath the weight of animals I couldn't see and sounds I couldn't name – chirps, whistles; screeches, caws – all was cool and serene. Deep lungfuls of lush air left me lightheaded. I reached out, running my hands through shafts of sunlight on their way to sparkle in the water at my feet.

My hands found the firm holds of small trees and moist, root-filled dirt. I scurried up the rise. When I was high enough to see out of the ravine, I reached to scramble up over the ridge. The dirt was sandy. Chunks crumbled around my fingers. Losing my balance, I dug deeper to keep from falling into the air behind me. I found my grip, but not before pulling an anthill, with hundreds of fire ants, down upon me.

White-hot punctures covered my torso. My body flushed throughout. My face and fingers swelled. Stripping to the waist, I rolled around in the dust to try to sweep the anger of the ants away. My insides were one insistent throb trapped in a fast-ripening berry of skin. I sat up in the dirt to pull off my boots and my socks. A line of saliva streamed from my numbed mouth.

I awoke on the concrete patio of the orphanage being shot with epinephrine. The angry red bumps subsided, and the swelling stopped.

The next day we boated to an island off the coast. There was snorkeling, hiking, a zip line, a grand spread of local seafood, fresh-cut fruit, an open bar. I dove from the boat, snorkeling through clear ocean.

I left the water hungry and made my way to the food – and drink. I was an eighteen-year-old with a known history of substance abuse left alone with something I should not have been.

A girl I had a thing for, Corrine, told me that the tour-guide, who'd repeatedly checked her zip-line harness, had used the occasion to feel her up. I didn't have the nerve to accuse a grown man, face-to-face, of molesting my friend, but when the comment cards were handed out on the bus ride over dilapidated roads, I filled mine out in detail.

I don't remember what I wrote, but soon the guide was storming through the bus demanding to know the author of the words on the crumpled paper in his hand. I spoke out.

The trip director, whom I'd respected, all but called me a liar. When Corrine backed me up I felt vindicated, proud: a victory. But an adult had eavesdropped on me whispering against him with a friend.

We gathered at the evening service on the patio that evening to decide how to move forward together in the Spirit of Christ. The group prayed over me, words moving from one to another, some talking from the heart, others chattering in low, nonsense tongues filling the night air, noise of life a contrast to the dark beyond.

The men encircled me, laying their hands on my arms, shoulders, head. My back, blistered from the sun, begged away from the chair. Their grip tightened. I wasn't weak. I began to struggle. The scraping pain rung out across my skin. My vision clouded with tears. I sank down in the chair, using the armrest to scrape all the fingers loose, and broke free till one of them tripped me.

In an instant, the men had collapsed in upon me. My blisters burst and my skin screamed. They sat on my legs, held my feet, kneeled on my arms to hold me in place.

The women held hands in a ring about us. Their lilting voices rose and fell in prayers and song.

The men shouted as if at demons, pounding fists upon my chest in command of a spirit not there, snarling demands in my face, clutching fistfuls of hair to shake my head before casting it back against the concrete where they'd trapped me. The hollow thud of their blows shook my ribs and traveled up into my skull. I drifted in and out of consciousness during the hours that followed. Sometime in the early morning, they grew tired and dragged me to a room, where they abandoned me.

It has been more than twenty years since I lay in that room without light. In another twenty years I hope to look back and feel as far away from who I am now, as I feel today from that kid: a boy in flames.

I believe the ultimate duty of a writer is to channel truth. Recently, however, I've come to understand that truth is more than factual accuracy; it is a connection of resonance between reader and author, a deep recognition of something kindred in other people's stories. So, then, is a pseudo-journalist exposing someone's embarrassing secrets across the pages of a tabloid something we can call truth? I don't think so. I've committed myself to telling truth that uplifts, inspires, ignites, or at the very least entertains without preying on the soft target humanity.

**—Benjamin Frandsen**

*Honorable Mention, Nonfiction*

*from*

# On a Railroad

## (Soo-Line)
## MARK ALTENHOFEN

In most places the tracks would have divided the town into the haves and have-nots. But in ours that wasn't so. Only two houses stood on the far side. We viewed ourselves as better off than those who lived close to the Kraft plant, in the trailer park, or in the "governmentals"—apartments subsidized by the state welfare office—though for Sunday lunch we ate noodles with butter and ketchup sandwiches like the rest.

The two Eriks, Craig, Charlie and I hunted, fished, camped together whenever we could. Summer nights were spent playing kick-the-can and ghost in the graveyard until we couldn't see and our parents rounded us up with flashlights. Winter days were for sledding and snow forts.

Sometimes others would drift into our group, like Eggy—for Greg, which his baby brother was not able to pronounce. Six years older, he was master of arcade games, his initials dominating the top scores for Mario Brothers and Donkey Kong. Regardless of age, though, we shared one obsession: the Soo-Line tracks.

There we found cigarettes, half-empty whiskey bottles, and tin cans to recycle in hopes of buying new hockey skates. To the east, in Schwinghammer Lake, we'd find fish waiting for our hooks; to the west, plump cornfields and woodlots where pheasant, rabbit, and squirrel for the family freezer. Our forts and hideaways were along the tracks, most often in the densest brush we could penetrate. When Charlie won his first brand-new bike ever at the church raffle we gave him a soda shower there, orange pop and cola cascading from his dark curls as we cheered his good luck. When I was nine, after my father's funeral my friends found me there, half frozen in our fort. The tears threatened to freeze to our cheeks that December day.

Some places have, for kids, a kind of wild magic. That magic requires sacrifice to keep it strong: the hours you spend in the tree fort, the baseballs you can never find in the tall grass field, the fearful glances you offer the house on the corner. For us it was mainly lost change, broken toys, the time Erik R. sprained his ankle, or when Craig pancaked the wheel of his bike and knocked himself out. Craig's dog Petey was killed on the tracks. We buried his broken body – fluffy white fur matted and his blue eyes clouded – beneath the raspberry bush where we found him. We made a cross for him and Eggy—used a wood-burner to etch Petey's name. For others, the cost was steeper. Two people committed suicide there. We put little crosses by the orange spray-paint used to mark the bodies. Out of respect, we avoided those areas, but didn't avoid the tracks.

Charlie, Craig, the two Eriks, and I learned to read the signs that the Beast was on its way. As it roared past, its breath sucking at our clothes, we'd speculate upon where it had been, what it had seen, where it was bound. We knew the names of towns the Beast passed through, but not what was beyond them.

One June morning, when the crappies and the sunnies were sure to bite, Eggy came to collect us. We'd spent the night watching Friday the 13th and declined the five a.m. invitation. Instead, Eggy's little sister Jenny went with him. The best place to find fish in the morning was directly beneath the trestle bridge.

Jenny didn't know the Soo-Line, didn't know the tricks and games. If we had gone, we'd have put the pop can on the tracks as alert. Or one of us would have looked up. We knew the Beast's schedule: every other Sunday, plus the third Saturday of every month, although the timetable had changed just then.

Jenny said that Eggy's foot got stuck between two ties.

Charlie, Craig and I walked the tracks one last time to Schwinghammer Lake. We set a soda on the rail—no telling, now, with the beast, until we found the orange paint and dug a grave, for Eggy.

Instead of a cross we planted a seedling tree, and in the hole beneath it laid a set of fish hooks and three quarters. We didn't completely avoid the Soo-Line afterward—still a convenient short-cut from one side of the town to the other. But the wild magic had asked too much this time.

*Honorable Mention, Nonfiction*

*from*

# Regret's Tragic Romance

## A Little Girl's Journey from Failure to Forgiveness and Freedom

## ANNAMARIE HARRIS ROMERO

I remember running off, carrying my fishing pole and not really paying any attention to my surroundings. As I rounded a slight bend I tripped, sending my fishing pole flying ahead of me. It looked like the pole was resting on solid ground, so I jumped up to reach for my pole. As I did, the ground gave way beneath me and I felt myself plummeting straight down. I can still see the green, murky water and the bubbles rising around me as I began sinking. I'll never forget the stench of that stagnant moss infested lake water. It engulfed my nasal passages and began entering my lungs. I frantically flailed my arms and legs in a panicked attempt to get my head back above the surface of the water.

That's when everything went blank. The next thing I recall is coming to on the bank of the lake surrounded by a group of unfamiliar faces including the man whom I later found out had just saved my life. I was relieved to see my father and couldn't wait for him to grab me, and hold me, and tell me how sorry he was that he hadn't watched me closer. Instead he yelled at me! He told me I had no business running off like that, and asked me if I understood that I could have died?

It was definitely not the reaction I expected; and for a little girl who was scared and searching for reassurance, it is not only painful, but devastating, to hear your daddy is mad at you at the very moment you need him most.

I allowed a singular, unfair reaction from my father to damage my willingness and possibly my ability to trust people for almost one-half of my adult life. I was always waiting for that proverbial "other shoe" to drop. I believe I was subconsciously searching for the pivotal moment in any given situation where my reality would suddenly fall short of my expectations and I would once again be left disappointed and confused.

Thanks to an ironic and almost tragic twist of fate, I was given an emotional insight into what my father may have been feeling that day at the lake so long ago.

At the time I was a single mom with six daughters and an infant grandson to take care of. Due to my lack of finances, opportunities to go somewhere and do something fun with these children were limited. It was a very hot day, and the girls and I decided to make a picnic lunch and go down to the river to cool off. Even though I do not care for natural bodies of water (as you can imagine) I reasoned that the water was fairly shallow and moving slowly; so I figured, "What could go wrong?" At the river, the older girls were floating on an inner tube, splashing around and having fun. I was a little way downstream walking in the cool water holding my nine-month old grandson, enjoying the scenery when what still seems like a surreal and improbable accident occurred. I slipped on the slimy rocks on the riverbed! I fell and somehow my shoulder got wedged beneath a piece of large tree limb that had broken into the water. I was holding the baby above the water even though my face was five to six inches below the surface. I was lying on my back, staring up at my grandson as I prayed that the Lord would not allow my strength to give out before someone saved this precious child, I have no idea how long I held Jayden above me or how long I spent underwater. I vaguely remember him being lifted out of my arms, and then nothing. For the second time in my life I woke up, lying on the bank of a body of water, confused, scared, and basically traumatized. The first thing I did when I awoke was to check about his condition. I was told that not only was he just fine, but somehow he had barely gotten damp.

The second thing I did, once I knew things were all right, was scream. In those stress filled moments, as the realization of what potentially could have occurred began to sink in, my perspective changed. My eyes and heart were essentially opened that day. I gained much needed clarity into what my poor father may have felt that day once he realized that I was okay. I suddenly understood that it wasn't me he was mad at. He reacted the way he did, not because he didn't care, but because he cared so much!

*Fielding A. Dawson Prize in Nonfiction*

*from*

# The Box

## *(The True Account of My First Thirty Days in Solitary Confinement)*
## DERICK MCCARTHY

"Maybe the box isn't going to be as bad as I thought it would be," I said to myself as I laid back on my bed.

Unfortunately, that couldn't be further from the truth.

A few days had passed and I had gotten used to the workings of the box. It was a daily routine of the same thing: breakfast at 6 a.m., recreation at 7 a.m., showers at 8 a.m., lunch at 11 a.m., take a nap at 12 p.m., mail at 2 p.m. and dinner at 5 p.m. The only thing that would change up the monotony of this routine were the visits that occurred Wednesday and Thursday evenings and Friday, Saturday and Sunday mornings.

When you first arrive in the box you must do something called getting your weight up, which is essentially having clout. In the beginning, the C.O.s don't know you, so they'll shit on you; this is called not having your weight up. You'll come out last for the showers or you might not get one, you'll get the phone last, you won't go to rec or your food tray might contain a small portion of food or be cold, plus a lot of other disrespectful things that might happen when you deal with a C.O. Getting your weight up is not hard to do but it is not easy either; everyone in the box does not have or will not get their weight up. Getting your weight up has to do with a combination of things. First, the guys who have been in the box the longest or those who already have their weight up must jack you. Jack is a term that we use to express that we accept and respect another person and/or their actions, i.e. I jack the way he is handling that. The C.O.s must see that other people with their weight up jack you. The SPA (Suicide Prevention Aide) and other inmates must jack you. You must make small talk with other C.O.s so that they can jack you also. Secondly, you must not tolerate any disrespect from anyone. Any aggression or disrespect toward you from another inmate or C.O. must be handled swiftly and possibly with violence. You can accomplish this in a few days, a few weeks or a few months, but once you are jacked, you have started to get your weight up. There are other ways to get your weight up, but these are the most common.

There are different levels to having your weight up: the first level is having your weight up a little bit, meaning you can do a little bit of things like get the phone next if certain people aren't waiting for it, maybe a little extra food on your tray (if it is available), and a few other small things. This level is normally achieved by association, hanging with someone with their weight up. The second level is having your weight half way up, meaning you can pick what shower you want to go into, the SPA comes when you call him, you might be given some drugs if they're in the housing unit, you'll get extra food on your tray unless the food amount is short, you'll be able to have your whip and a few other things. The third level is having your weight all the way up, which means you do whatever you want. The C.O.s come when you call them, you can pick when and what shower you'll get in, you'll always have extra food, even when it's short they'll call the mess hall to get you more, you get the phone exactly when you want it, no matter who had next, they'll wake you up to go to rec, you'll go to the barbershop every week, when they search your cell they will not take anything from you, the SPA will cook for you, everyone, even Captains, stop at your cell to talk to you, and you receive some of every drug in that comes into the house. Basically, you run the place.

About two weeks had passed and little by little, I had started to get my weight up. I started being able to pick the shower I wanted to use. I would get a little extra food on my tray, and I wouldn't get skipped for the phone. The C.O.s were even starting to jack me.

# Acknowledgments

We've learned that it takes an entire village to create a book of this scope. Thank you, first and foremost, to the dedicated PEN America Prison Writing Committee who contributed tireless hours and energy, pouring through hundreds of manuscripts in order to arrive at the work you see here.

Thank you to those who made this book beautiful: Molly Crabapple for a gorgeous original cover illustration, made expressly for this anthology, and our multi-talented colleague Nadxi Nieto for aesthetic guidance in cover design. To Illustrated PEN editors Robert Kirby, Meg Lemke, Dave Ortega and Whit Taylor for curating a special feature focused on the work of our Prison Writing Contest, and to the contributing artists for exciting visual responses to our writer's work.

Thank you to following PEN Prison Writing Program Mentors who did an excellent job editing the Honorable Mention excerpts, as well as stage-ready excerpts of all award-winning work: Jaclyn Alexander, Ryan Blacketter, Eric Boyd, Anderson Cook, Tony Hughes, Laurie McMillan, Simon Phillips, Elizabeth Poreba, Shelley Salamensky, Douglas Silver, Ran Walker, Gary Winter and Danielle Zuckerman.

Thank you to Beth Mannion, Giselle Elizabeth Robledo and Alan Yount for support on transcribing the original typed hard copy and handwritten submissions sent to us in the mail. Thank you to Juliann Nelson, PEN America's Web Editor, and her interns Stephan Kozub and Anna Russian for sharp copyediting.

Thank you to Jennifer Bowen Hicks, Piper Kerman, Keise Laymon, Aja Monet, and Jeffery Toobin for such wonderful words to brag with.

Thank you to all of our tremendous colleagues at PEN America, and special gratitude to Dru Menaker, Chief Operating Officer and Suzanne Nossel, Chief Executive Officer, for leadership, and enthusiastic support of our program.

Thank you to our program funder and the individual donors and PEN America members who have earmarked contributions for our Prison Writing Program— you made all of this possible.

Extra special thanks to Sarah Faure, Christina John, Grace Kearney, Ezra Kohn and Miranda Levingston, our Spring and Summer 2018 Prison Writing

Program Interns who transcribed, answered letters, filed contest entries, offered ideas, guidance—and so much more.

*And finally, we know from our own experience that it takes a whole lot of guts and courage to risk rejection when submitting for publication. Thank you to all the writers who send work to our contest. Thank you for allowing us the opportunity to step into the worlds you live in, and create on the page. Please keep submitting to us—and everywhere.*

CPSIA information can be obtained
at www.ICGtesting.com
Printed in the USA
FSHW022104080121
77540FS